Good Drinks

Good Drinks

Alcohol-Free Recipes for When You're Not Drinking for Whatever Reason

Julia Bainbridge

Photographs by Alex Lau

TEN SPEED PRESS
California | New York

For Katie

and for anyone trying to do it differently

Contents

Intro-
duction

Of Me

I spent the summer of 2018 crisscrossing the country in my (some-what) dependable 2006 Subaru Impreza. After a decade of writing about food and drinks in New York City and two years doing the same in Atlanta, I got a book deal—for this very book!—and I decided that the best way to do research was to put my foot on the gas and go.

I was in search of alcohol-free mixed drinks at a time when, serendipitously, they were starting to be taken more seriously. Bartenders were (and still are) pushing against the boundaries that had previously limited "mocktails" to syrup-laden juices or glo-rified Shirley Temples, and consumers—sober or not—were getting curious. I knew I wouldn't be writing the first book on nonalcoholic drinks, but I also knew that my work could capitalize on this new-found acceptance and energy. And because I was finding the things I *really* wanted to drink in bars, restaurants, and cafés as opposed to in other books, I could tap the people whose job it is to make good, balanced beverages—no matter the alcohol content.

You could say I did a lot of drinking and driving that summer.

In between interviews and states, my car's (painfully out-dated) sound system stayed silent as I mulled over pieces of this book. How odd, my friend Tunde commented, that I could drive for hours with no music. But I needed the quiet to think, as I moved along: "Which of these beverages are still on my mind days after tasting them? Which recipes feel fresh? Which drinks warrant the effort they take to make? How much of this book is about the drinks and how much of it is about me?"

Somewhere in New Mexico, I decided that all you really need to know about my relationship to alcohol is that I'm trying not to drink it—at least not for a good while. More important: I like to eat delicious things, I like to drink delicious things, and I like to do both with the people I love. There are many others like me, and the rea-sons they don't drink booze vary: religion, health issues, substance use disorders, pregnancy, mindful living. Maybe alcohol simply doesn't fit into their lives anymore. Maybe they're just not drinking this week. Or this night. Or this hour. (I know plenty of people who switch back and forth between alcoholic and nonalcoholic drinks throughout the course of a Saturday night out.) Some statistics show that Americans are consuming less alcohol than they used to, and I hope that what I discovered on the road will get them into the kitchen. (Because it's not about the bar; at home, good nonalcoholic drinks are made in the kitchen. More on that later.)

In Denver, Death & Co's bartenders showed me how kefir whey gives body to nonalcoholic drinks (see page 92), which can be lacking in that area. Jermaine Whitehead handed me his recipe for the Rockefeller (page 166) from across the bar at Deep Dive in Seattle, and upon reading it, I realized I was going to have to dig through my spice cabinet, break out my 4-quart saucepan, and turn on the stove. (It ended up being worth it.) I sat in Gabriella Mlynarczyk's living room in Los Angeles while she pressed watermelon juice with mint, rose water, and pickled plum vinegar. (Find a similar recipe of Gaby's on page 66.) The next day, I drove back east thinking about that sweet, tart, saline drink, my tongue watering. And yes, that trip was quiet, too.

"I think I understand the driving-in-silence thing," Tunde told me, once the trip was over. "Been walking in silence recently. It's amazing."

Now, though, it's time to make noise. These drinks deserve a party.

Of the Drinks

I saw all kinds of terms applied to this category of drinks on my trip across America: Alcohol-Free Cocktails, Virgin Cocktails (ick), Teetotalers, Soft Drinks (don't hate it), Temperance Drinks (pretentious!), Zero-Proof Cocktails, Neutral Cocktails (hmm?), 0% ABV Drinks, the list goes on. The good thing is, people are trying to come up with something to replace Mocktail, which, while effective in its simplicity and ubiquity, feels juvenile to me. And as Chicago bar owner Julia Momose wrote in her manifesto against the word, there's an air of disappointment to it. Mocktail implies that the drink is a lesser version of the "real" thing: a cocktail with alcohol in it.

Julia, whose recipe you can find on page 140, proposes the term Spiritfree. "There's something lighthearted and intentional about the name Spiritfree," she wrote. "It's not holding back, nor is it being held back." My approach is to sidestep the debate and perhaps defiantly call them Drinks. Good Drinks. That wouldn't be fair in a bar, of course, because patrons deserve clarity; but this is a book and its subject is unambiguous.

So! Let's have a drink—a good one.

How This Book Is Structured

Could the recipes in this book have been organized by drink style: sour, fizz, highball, cobbler, and so on? Sort of. Those labels pertain to cocktails, and these drinks don't fit squarely into the same families. What about a looser style categorization: long drinks, short drinks, et cetera? Maybe. Or grouped by base ingredient: tea, coffee, milk, juice? That wouldn't be the sexiest approach, in my opinion, but one could take it.

Letting the drink itself drive structure isn't a bad idea, but I'm more inspired by occasion. My cravings usually start with a situation, a mood, a vibe, an atmosphere. So, my goal is to give you ideas for what to drink during your leisure time: over brunch, on lazy weekend afternoons, at happy hour, with leisurely dinners, and after dinner, when you're capping the night with friends or reflecting on the day in solitude. As a *bonne vivante* who wants to be *vivante* without alcohol, this is the most useful organizing principle to me, and I hope it works for you, too.

Often these occasions are social gatherings, so, when possible, I've included instructions for how to batch the drinks in order to serve a group. And because I want to give you both easy-to-execute ideas as well as more involved ones, the recipes range in terms of difficulty, which I've indicated with a Commitment Level rating. (More on that on page 13.) Peppered throughout the book are long quotes from food and drinks writers, bartenders, and restaurateurs who frankly couldn't shut up (!) about their favorite drinks. I decided to get them on the record, to capture their excitement and give you another handful of ideas.

Something else I'll note here because I can't figure out where else to slot it: For those of you who might be cutting back on alcohol for fitness reasons, know that some of these recipes happen to be low on sugar and calories, but many are not. These drinks aren't for cleansing, they're for pleasure—which comes, in this case, not from an altered state of mind, but from flavor (and perhaps the charm of holding an elegant glass). Many of those flavors are mature; others would feel at home at an old-fashioned soda fountain. I like it all.

Finally, as much as I've endeavored to give you variety here, this book is not exhaustive. These fifty-some recipes don't reflect each and every corner of today's alcohol-free beverage landscape, but they are the best drinks I tasted during my research. In other words, there's a lot more drinking to be done! So please use the following pages not only as a guide for what to drink, but also as a literal guidebook: Visit these bars and restaurants during your travels and see what they're offering. Then ask their bartenders who else in town makes great nonalcoholic drinks, because I'm sure that since this book went to print, many places either have opened or have decided to dedicate more of their beverage menu real estate to serving you. Maybe, just maybe, you'll taste something completely new. You just have to promise to tell me about it. (I'm @juliabainbridge on Twitter and Instagram.)

On Making Good Drinks

It can be difficult to snap a backbone onto a mixed drink without wine or spirits. Alcohol provides structure and complexity, and it's often pleasantly bitter and bracing. Remove it from a cocktail, and you're left with sugar, acid, and some cold water.

I found different approaches to building nonalcoholic drinks when I was on the road. Some bartenders make alcohol-free versions of classic cocktails. At first I bristled at this: "Why do we have to call it a NOgroni? Why can't it be a fully formed drink of its own?" I came around, in some cases. It makes sense to step back from a Negroni and, instead of trying to re-create it exactly (a recipe for failure), consider the Negroni experience. It's sweet up front, then bitter and dry at the back. It tastes of stewed plums and rhubarb and vanilla and bitter orange. That can be delivered without alcohol. Plus, classic cocktail making is mainly about balancing flavors. The tension between sweet, sour, salty, bitter, and umami is what the palate wants in a drink, whether it contains alcohol or not.

Then there are those for whom classic drink templates do not apply. For them, alcohol isn't the crux of the drink, squash is. Or jasmine tea is. Or rosemary is. "It's not about making a drink minus booze," says Ryan Chetiyawardana, who owns restaurants in London, Amsterdam, and Washington, D.C., and is one of the world's most influential bartenders. "It's about taking the care to make a balanced drink, and it happens not to have booze."

Both schools of thought are reflected here, and while some recipes are easily accessible, for others, you're going to have to order gentian root and raspberry vinegar. Then, you're going to have to roll up your sleeves and hone your chef's knife. Hopefully, as more sophisticated products come onto the market, you'll be able to do more opening and pouring and less sourcing, slicing, steeping, and juicing; but I, for one, like the tinkering. Until recently, nonalcoholic mixed drinks have been treated as afterthoughts. A higher level of effort and care anoints them as proper drinks. Good Drinks.

And, hey: If you put in the work, you might even enjoy your drink more. "The IKEA Effect," a 2011 study published by researchers from Harvard Business School, Tulane University, and Duke University showed that when participants in the study assembled IKEA boxes, folded origami, or built sets of Legos themselves, they valued the end product more highly than when others did the work for them. What's more, the study shows that effort without completion does not increase valuation. So stick with it!

All of that said, if you don't want to remove the zest from eight oranges, eight lemons, and four grapefruits and steep them in water with nutmeg and cloves for forty-five minutes, I understand. I love seltzer water with a dash of bitters, too. But I'm guessing that if you picked up this book, you're game to play around in the kitchen if it means ultimately enjoying a balanced beverage—and, in some cases, a real culinary experience.

It's *fun*. Remember that? That's what I'm after.

"Alcohol-Free," Explained

Very few of us consume zero alcohol. One 1990 USDA study tested a variety of orange juices and found them to contain anywhere between 0.008% and 0.09% alcohol by volume (ABV). "Nonalcoholic is a little bit of an abstract concept," says Sandor Katz, author of *The Art of Fermentation*. "In the world of carbohydrates, it barely exists."

That said, the U.S. Congress considers beverages that measure 0.5% ABV and above to be alcoholic. Beer and wine labeled nonalcoholic, as well as kombucha available for purchase by minors at grocery stores, must all come in at below 0.5% ABV—so this is the number many nondrinkers use as their cutoff, too.

The funny thing is, that number has nothing to do with how alcohol affects the human body or mind, and everything to do with federal revenue. With the help of Jarrett Dieterle and Kevin Kosar at the public policy research organization R Street Institute in Washington, D.C. (hi, guys!), I dug around in the legislative history. We read the Alcoholic Beverage Labeling Act (1988), which led us to the Volstead Act (1919), which implemented Prohibition, sure that we would find a satisfactory explanation of the number. Most everywhere, the figure "one-half of one per cent" appears next to a discussion of taxation, without any real reasoning.

Eventually, we found an article published in the *Harvard Crimson* in May 1920. Titled "Why 1-2 of One Percent," it was written by William E. Johnson, one of the foremost advocates of Prohibition. Johnson was supposedly the one who came up with the 0.5% ABV level, and though clearly biased, even he admits toward the end of the paper: "It is not a question as to whether one-half of one per cent is intoxicating or whether even two per cent is intoxicating, it is only a question of the adequate enforcement of any law prohibiting the manufacture and sale of intoxicating liquors." He claimed that the threshold had previously been set at 2% ABV, but that "defiant brewers" marketed their products as below 2% ABV when they were, in fact, much higher. Former New Jersey governor Walter E. Edge thought that 3% ABV would have been a more reasonable number. (He wrote about that as well as the failure of the Volstead Act in a 1923 article called "The Non-Effectiveness of the Volstead Act." I appreciate a straightforward title!)

There's no clear scientific basis for 0.5% ABV to be the line of demarcation, as far as I can tell.

Hannah Crum, president and cofounder of Kombucha Brewers International (KBI), thinks it's painfully outdated, anyway. According to her, the alcohol present in raw kombucha is not only a preservative but also helps deliver a matrix of vital nutrients to its consumer. "But, being a country of extremes, we've never really landed anywhere in the middle," she says. Crum and other KBI members have initiated the Keeping Our Manufacturers from Being Unfairly Taxed While Championing Health Act (KOMBUCHA),

Commitment Level

To make things easier, I've assessed the difficulty of each recipe and assigned it a rating accordingly. That way, you can get an immediate sense of what each drink requires without having to read the full recipe. Save the labor-intensive projects for when you have the time and energy and go for lower effort when you want a quicker fix.

Here's how I define each Commitment Level:

● ○ ○ ○

You're either cooking a syrup *or* using your juicer *or* marinating or infusing something. The rest of the prep is pretty easy stuff like juicing citrus.

● ● ○ ○

There's more time involved, but it's not complicated. You're either cooking a syrup, brewing a tea, or blending and straining something. In addition to that, the recipe might call for an ingredient that you have to order online or find at a specialty grocer or it might call for a piece of special equipment.

● ● ● ○

There are two subrecipes, plus you might have to source a special ingredient.

● ● ● ●

This is a weekend project, for which you have to source a number of ingredients and spend some serious time in the kitchen.

a bill that would raise the taxation point for kombucha from 0.5% to 1.25% ABV. "Since compliance is the name of the game, we've gone straight to the Internal Revenue Code to make a commonsense update. We believe the law never intended to tax traditionally fermented, low-alcohol beverages like they do beer." As of this book's printing, KOMBUCHA is sitting with Congress.

If it were possible to settle on a "nonintoxicating" demarcation, that would, in my opinion, make a lot more sense than "nonalcoholic." But as long as 0.5% ABV is the law, that's what will govern this book.

Fermented Drinks

Fermentation, an ancient form of food alchemy that bestowed wine on the world, has become trendy today. More and more people are getting turned on to the pungent aromas and tangy flavors that microorganisms, when left to do their things, pull out of carbohydrates, and recipes for kimchi, kefir, miso, and sauerkraut can all be found on the pages of in-vogue culinary magazines.

The most popular of the more lightly fermented beverages is kombucha, which is made with tea, sugar, a SCOBY (symbiotic culture of bacteria and yeast), and a little bit of time. You'll notice, though, that there are no recipes for kombucha in this book. I love the funk that fermentation brings, but you know what else comes along with the process? Alcohol. And while the alcohol in kombucha is generally self-limiting—the yeast feeds on sugar and produces ethanol, while bacteria simultaneously consume that ethanol and convert it to organic acids—it does have the potential to get above 1% ABV in a home environment. (Remember, I'm going with the 0.5% ABV rule.)

I tested some simpler yeast fermentations such as tepache, a pineapple drink from Mexico, and I considered running those recipes with a disclaimer to consume on the shorter end of the fermentation process, before the drinks reached above 0.5% ABV. But, again, conditions are hard to control outside of a laboratory-like production facility. The sugar content of the fruit and the temperature of your home, among other factors, affect the rate of fermentation and, thus, the production of alcohol. In other words, I can't guarantee that what happened in my kitchen would happen in yours. It likely wouldn't.

Harold McGee, one of our country's top food science writers, ultimately put it to me this way: "The transformations that make these drinks what they are, are predicated on alcohol being produced. I would rule them out, just on that very basic ground." And so I did.

Bitters

Bitters are an aromatic and, yes, often bitter liquid seasoning. Historically, this infusion of roots, barks, spices, herbs, and other botanicals was consumed for its medicinal properties; then sometime in the eighteenth century, Americans took to mixing it into cocktails. Brad Thomas Parsons's comprehensive *Bitters: A Spirited History of a Classic Cure-All* gets into the details, but for our purposes, all you need to know is that the United States had a bitters boom in the early aughts and now there are a zillion flavors and brands from which to choose.

Most of them are made with alcohol, since it's such an effective extractor of flavor, but because the Alcohol and Tobacco Tax and Trade Bureau (TTB) considers bitters to be a food item, they're not subject to the labeling requirements that TTB enforces. (It's a different story for potable bitters such as Campari and Aperol, which are regulated as distilled spirits products.) In other words, makers aren't required to disclose the ABV of their bitters on the bottle. Some do, though, in the name of transparency.

Even Fee Brothers bitters, which many believe are alcohol-free because their base is glycerin, not high-proof vodka or some other neutral grain spirit, actually do contain alcohol. This is because, instead of working with raw ingredients, the company purchases extracts from four flavor houses, and those extracts are made with alcohol. Joe Fee, who along with his sister Ellen was a fourth-generation operator of the family business, told me that their bitters can contain anywhere from around 2% to 36% ABV, depending on the recipe.

Here's why I bring all of this up: Some recipes in this book call for bitters. Ultimately, because you're using only a couple dashes in a drink, the amount of alcohol you're ingesting is statistically insignificant.

Let's use Angostura bitters as an example: The bottle I'm looking at right now measures 44.7% ABV. If one standard dash equals ⅛ teaspoon, and 1 ounce equals 6 teaspoons, then a 5-ounce glass of, say, iced tea topped with three dashes of Angostura bitters is about 0.56% alcohol. Yes, that is technically what the law considers to be alcoholic, but (1) only by a hair and (2) as we discussed earlier, this number has little if nothing to do with intoxication. To put this into perspective, the National Institutes of Health considers a standard glass of wine to be 12% alcohol. It's also worth knowing that most alcohol-based bitters ring in at somewhere between 35% and 45% ABV, so Angostura is on the high end.

Having said all of this, I know some nondrinkers for whom this is a problem. If you're in their camp, please either choose a bitter labeled with a lower percentage of ABV than Angostura's, reduce the number of dashes in your drink, sub in a nonalcoholic bitter, or skip those recipes entirely.

Which brings me to the two commercial brands of bitters I know of that are completely devoid of alcohol. One is Dram, based in Salida, Colorado. Co-owner Shae Whitney says she uses glycerin and raw ingredients, a process that limits her. "Fruits are pretty impossible to penetrate, so we don't make peach or cherry bitters, for example," she says. "It's hard to get delicate flavors into glycerin." Currently, she sells bitters flavored with palo santo; citrus; lavender–lemon balm; sage; one she calls "black," which is a combination of black cardamom, black tea, black currants, and black walnuts; and an aromatic bitter made with ginger, fennel, cinnamon, and herbs. Find them—I bought them all!—at dramapothecary.com.

Unlike Dram, El Guapo, based in New Orleans, Louisiana, does use ethanol to extract flavor from certain ingredients, but owner Christa Cotton evaporates the alcohol before mixing the flavors with vegetable-based glycerin and bottling the bitters. "All of our SKUs are 0% ABV when they hit store shelves," she says. You can buy her Good Food Award–winning chicory pecan bitters, among others, at elguapobitters.com.

For DIY nonalcoholic bitters, find Washington, D.C.–based bartender Hunter Douglas's recipe on page 115.

Tools

Remember: You are going to cook in order to make these drinks! It's important to have a cutting board, a sharp chef's knife, a 4-quart saucepan, measuring cups, and storage containers. Beyond those things, here are the tools that will make your life easier, starting with the ones I reach for most often. They're important pieces of equipment to have if you want to execute these recipes successfully.

Jigger

A jigger is basically a mini measuring cup that you can grasp with your fingers. When I started testing recipes for this book, I was a snob for stainless steel. (If you like the look of that smooth metal, too, go for it, but I recommend a double-sided version that measures 1 ounce on one side and 2 ounces on the other, with etched lines demarcating 1/4 and/or 1/2 ounce.) As time wore on, I kept reaching for OXO's mini angled measuring cup. It's clear plastic, so you can see the liquid inside, and it has a spout, which helps reduce spillage. (If you absolutely *must*, 1 ounce is equal to 2 tablespoons, but jiggers are cheap and useful, so you should only use measuring spoons in a pinch.)

Shaker

There are a number of makes and models, but I recommend a fully metal Boston shaker. Learning how to successfully fit the two tins together and separate them takes practice, but this version is unbreakable (compared to the tin-on-glass Boston) and simple (two pieces compared to the Cobbler shaker's three).

Strainers

The Julep strainer is mostly used for stirred drinks; it's basically a wide spoon with holes. A Hawthorne strainer is similar, but the paddle is flat and rimmed with small coils, which help trap bits of things that shaking a drink might produce. If you don't want to buy both, the Hawthorne works for everything. (You don't really *need* a Julep strainer.)

Sometimes, you'll use a small mesh strainer (a tea strainer is fine) in conjunction with the Hawthorne; that's called a "double strain."

You'll also want a chinois or some other deep, conical, fine-meshed sieve for straining larger quantities of fruit purees or "cooked" items.

Peeler

A Y-peeler is, hands down, superior to a straight swivel peeler. (You can fight me on this; I'm ready! Remember: @juliabainbridge on Twitter and Instagram.) Its wide handle makes it easier to hold, and the position of the blade makes it…it's just better! Brand-wise, I'm with Kuhn Rikon; it's cheap and the carbon steel blade stays sharp for a good while.

Juicers

You'll need two pieces of equipment: (1) For citrus fruits, use a hinged hand press, preferably stainless steel. Or there's your actual hand, a tool most of us were lucky enough to be born with. (2) A machine that uses centrifugal force is essential, especially for more fibrous fruits and vegetables. Breville's Juice Fountain Elite is what I have at home, and while it's not inexpensive, it *is* everlasting.

Blender

You'll use a blender to puree softer fruits like ripe pears and melon and to, well, blend. You can't go wrong with pretty much any Vitamix blender, but they'll cost you. (Reconditioned models can be purchased for less.) Otherwise, just be sure to choose something that's sturdy and solidly built.

Carbonator

A SodaStream can add bubbles to water, tea, and other clear liquids as long as you're careful. The company doesn't recommend using the machine for anything other than water, and for good reason: If you clog its valve, the bottle can burst. To avoid this, fill it only one-third to one-half full. If you're serving a crowd, that means you'll have to carbonate in batches, but trust me that safety is key here. Watch closely as you work to make sure no foam reaches the top of the bottle. I also had better luck incorporating syrups after carbonation; you may lose some effervescence in the process, but the

SodaStream is happier this way. Another option, which I prefer, is an iSi soda siphon. The bubbles it produces are bigger and stronger than a SodaStream, but I would still recommend sweetening your liquids after carbonating them, because sugar produces foam. (There are tricks for carbonating your liquid with the syrup already incorporated *without* creating a foamy mess. Head to bartender Jeffrey Morgenthaler's website jeffreymorgenthaler.com and search "How to Use an iSi Soda Siphon to Carbonate Housemade Sodas.") Overall, in order to achieve optimal carbonation levels, use only super-chilled, clear (as in not cloudy) liquids.

Mixing Glass and Spoon
For stirred drinks, you'll want both a mixing glass and a barspoon. For the former, you could use a pint glass or a measuring cup, but I'm a sucker for the beauty of the heavy-bottomed, Yarai-etched crystal. For the latter, go with a proper metal barspoon with a long, spiraled handle if you want to get fancy, but I know one bartender who uses a chopstick. It just needs to help you stir.

Other Kitchenware
One recipe calls for an extra-special tool, without which it will be difficult to make: To properly blend, dilute, and chill the Don't Touch My Car Keys (page 86), you'll want either a spindle drink mixer (I have a Hamilton Beach DrinkMaster Classic) or a swizzle stick.

Lastly, you could buy a muddler, but I call for its use only a couple times. The butt end of a wooden spoon works just fine.

Glassware

In each recipe, I've suggested the type of glassware that best suits the drink. You can color outside the lines, though. I'm not precious.

Except when it comes to chilling your glassware! If you're serving a cold mixed drink, you really should stick your glass in the freezer for 30 minutes.

Okay, okay, I understand that sometimes (most of the time?) that kind of preparation isn't possible. On the following pages, I've chosen to remind you to chill your glasses only in the recipes for which this is a nonnegotiable. (It's just a few.)

Coupe

Flute

Snifter

Collins

Cordial

Wine

Rocks

Pint

Tulip

Pearl Diver

Nick & Nora

Ingredients

Few items in your fridge or pantry couldn't *somehow* be used in a drink. Pickle brine (page 85)? Tahini (page 81)? Miso (page 110)? Sesame oil (page 140)? Sure! The possibilities are limitless, so I'll let the recipes in this book educate you about what ingredients make sense together. Here, I'll just get into the most important basics to guide your shopping.

To Store in the Fridge

Citrus Juice
Aroma impacts taste. Any citrus fruit's essential oils are stored in its skin, and when you juice the fruit, you release those aromas into the liquid. So please make your own fresh lemon, lime, orange, and grapefruit juice. And please fine-strain that juice to remove any pulp. Pulp is not your friend!

Choose fruit that's plump and fragrant, with smooth, though not necessarily unblemished, skin. You *will* want unblemished skin when it comes to choosing citrus for garnishes, though, so think about both juicing and garnishing when you shop.

Other Juice
When a recipe calls for juice, it almost always means the fresh version. (Store-bought juices often contain additives and preservatives.)

The exception is pomegranate juice. Pomegranates are a pain to work with, you get a relatively low yield, and POM is perfectly good. And, fine, if you want to avoid working with whole beets (I get it—they're messy), R.W. Knudsen makes a good organic beet juice.

Some say that the juice from canned tomatoes is superior to the fresh stuff for Bloody Marys, and while I agree, when it's fighting alcohol for flavor space, I like how light and vegetal this book's version of the drink is when made with fresh tomato juice (page 47). In the end, it's up to you! But if you go fresh, again: Choose for plumpness and fragrance.

It's important to note here that produce varies. I have measured juice yields to the best of my ability, but different pears, for example, get you slightly different results. Maybe mine was juicier for Lord knows what reason. Unfortunately, I have not been able to strike a deal with Mother Nature. She is her own woman, so just use your best judgment at the store!

Soda Water

When I say soda water, I mean either club soda or seltzer. (There is some debate over whether doing so is correct, but that's what I'm doing!) Seltzer is simply water plus carbon dioxide (CO_2). Club soda is water plus CO_2 plus minerals (such as sodium bicarbonate, sodium chloride, potassium sulfate, or disodium phosphate). For that reason, club soda tends to taste slightly salty, while seltzer just tastes like water. (Although, I'll also offer that any water but distilled will contain at least *some* minerals affecting flavor in *some* way.) To the average palate, there's little perceivable difference between the two, so I feel confident saying that you can use them interchangeably. (This does not apply to sparkling mineral waters, which come from natural sources. Big flavor differences there.)

There are a *lot* of opinions about soda water brands. Taste them for yourself and see what you like best: higher salinity or neutrality of flavor; tiny, sharp bubbles or fat, mellow bubbles. Some recipes in this book call for specific brands of soda water based on bartenders' personal preferences. Feel free to follow that advice or not. Just make sure to store whatever you buy in the refrigerator, which will keep the carbonation alive longer. Using chilled soda water also slows the melting of ice, thereby slowing dilution.

The other option is to make your own seltzer. More on that in the Tools section (page 20).

Tonic Water

Tonic's defining ingredient, quinine, was historically used to treat malaria. This bark is what gives tonic water its bitterness, which is then balanced by sugar and citric acid.

Today, you can find small-batch premium tonics that are less saccharine than those that, full of corn syrup, feel almost *sticky*. Fentimans, Fever-Tree, East Imperial, and

Top Note tonic are some of my favorite makers, who also produce tonics flavored with rosemary and thyme, elderflower, and bitter lemon, to name a few. These are wonderful on their own as well as mixed into cocktails.

Dairy and Dairy-ish

The recipes in this book either call for milk or cream. The milk is whole, coconut, almond, or sweetened and condensed. You'll also find milk in fermented form, known as kefir.

The cream is heavy or coconut, and here's the thing to know about coconut cream: Some grocery stores sell it (I like the Native Forest or Thai Kitchen brand). Some do not. If that's the case in your store, buy a can of coconut milk, preferably full-fat, and chill it overnight in the refrigerator. The cream will rise to the top and harden, so that you can scoop it out and use it. (Reserve the watery liquid for another use.)

Overall, these ingredients add fat to a drink, which means (1) flavor and (2) a creamy texture.

Herbs

Herbs are essential to drink–making. Lemon thyme, for example, is lightly sour and plays well with beets, fennel, or ginger. Tarragon has a louder volume, so to speak, and can enliven a grapefruit and soda. Overall, herbs should be fresh and vibrant, not dried. (Some people have found uses for dried herbs in cocktails. I have not.)

Verjus

Verjus is the juice of grapes that aren't yet ripe enough for wine production. (Between three and five weeks before grapes are ready for harvesting, winemakers thin the vines so that the remaining grapes have a better chance of concentrating their sugars. The trim, in some cases, becomes verjus.) Red verjus is rich and stone fruit–like; white verjus is crisp and tart. Overall, verjus has a more mature vibe than plain-old grape juice. My favorite for drinking with tonic or soda water is a pinkish one produced by Noble Handcrafted, which can be purchased at mikuniwildharvest.com. Others worth tasting: both Montinore and Wölffer Estate's white verjus, and Canadian brand Minus 8's red verjus. For use in cocktails, Fusion makes a red and a white that both play well with other ingredients. Once opened, verjus will keep in the fridge for about a month.

To Store in the Pantry

Sweeteners

Different sugars vary in flavor, as do other sweeteners such as maple syrup and honey. They're primarily used to sweeten drinks, but they can also add body and carry other flavors, such as when you're making a compound syrup with herbs or spices. I've indicated the sweetener that works best in each recipe.

Spices

So important! Cayenne pepper gives you heat, pink peppercorns have bite, cloves are warming...Again, I'll get into the specific choices in the recipes, but here, I'll say: Mostly buy them whole; store them in air-tight containers in a coolish, dark place; and smell them every so often to make sure they're still potent.

Salt

Salt your cocktails! It brightens them and makes each ingredient taste more like itself. Many bartenders use a weak saline solution for control and consistency, but at home, I just throw a few granules into the shaker. If it's a drink with a salted rim, or if it already contains a sodium-heavy ingredient such as soy sauce, then I don't use any additional salt. Otherwise, you'll find a mixture of sea salts, flavored salts, and good old kosher in these recipes. Each has a distinct flavor profile.

Tea

Tea is an entire world unto itself; there are as many varieties as there are wine (if not more). Some are nutty (buckwheat), some are smoky (Lapsang Souchong), some are earthy (Oolong). Rooibos is woodsy and vanilla-like. (And, technically, rooibos isn't tea! It's a tisane, or herbal tea. But I'm going to go ahead and call all water infusions "teas.") Not only is the choice of tea going to affect your drink, but you can also play around with steeping time: Go longer to extract bitterness, or lightly brew green or herbal teas if you want ethereal, pretty flavors.

In general, it's best to purchase loose-leaf tea from a high-quality purveyor—your local tea shop, if you have one, or an online merchant such as Harney & Sons (harney.com). If you're purchasing tea in bags (less cost effective, but great in a pinch; just cut the bags open and pour out the tea leaves), shop for a brand that uses "full-leaf tea," such as Mighty Leaf, rather than one that sells "dust and fannings" from broken tea leaves.

Vinegars

This book contains recipes for drinking vinegars such as shrubs, which are syrups made from fruit or vegetables, vinegar, and sugar and then often mixed with soda water. But also consider sherry, rice, or apple cider vinegar, which you might have previously limited to the realm of salad dressings. Just a splash can season a cocktail and give it some edge.

Flower Waters

Orange flower and rose waters are common in Middle Eastern cooking, and they deserve a spot in your cocktail pantry, too. A little goes a long way, though: You're mainly using these hydrosols for their aroma.

Other Acids

A few recipes in this book use acids in their powdered form (see Apple & Miso on page 110, Cham-pine on page 127, and Tarragon Cider on page 145). They provide acidity without adding either volume or secondary citrus flavors that might, in some cases, distract from the core ingredients in your drink. Mixed together, tartaric and lactic acids impart a champagne-like flavor. Citric acid tastes like lemon (it's the primary acid in lemon juice), clean and sharp. And malic acid, which is found in apples as well as some champagnes, brings tartness. Find them all at modernistpantry.com.

Nonalcoholic Spirits

You don't often hear "distillation" used in a nonalcoholic context, but Seedlip is, in fact, a botanical-driven, sugar-free, alcohol-free, shelf-stable "spirit" produced in England via copper stills. Founder Ben Branson, who lives on the land his family has been farming for about 320 years, has developed a kind of bespoke maceration, distillation, and filtration process for each ingredient that goes into the three (so far) Seedlip products. (Branson does, by the way, use a low amount of alcohol to extract flavor, but he removes it before bottling. It's a processing aid, in other words, not an ingredient.) There's Garden 108, which tastes like peas, rosemary, and thyme; Spice 94, made with allspice, cardamom, grapefruit, and bitter barks; and Grove 42, which combines blood orange with ginger and lemongrass. Many other nonalcoholic spirits have come onto the market, some better than others, but Seedlip really blew this space open, and it's the most accessible brand in the United States for now.

Ice

Ice has three jobs, when it comes to cocktail-making: to chill, to dilute, and to ornament. The ice you use to make a drink, working ice, does the first two. The ice in your finished drink, let's call it presentation ice, does all three.

You'll find three types of presentation ice in this book: (1) Ice! If the recipe lists no other word before "ice," that means whatever you normally use for drinks is fine. I like 1- to 1¼ inch-square cubes. (2) A rock. This is a bigger cube, say 2 inches square. If you're meant to use it, the recipe will call for a "large ice cube." You can go for a spherical shape if you prefer. (3) Crushed. This almost snowy ice allows for a super-cold and diluted drink—both important when tempering the sweetness in multiple juices and syrups. You can make crushed ice by pounding at regular ice; you just need a canvas sack, a mallet of sorts, and some feelings to expunge.

Some bartenders prefer the porousness and chewability of pebble ice, also called nugget ice, to all others. You can't really make pebble ice without a machine, though. Appropriately sized trays exist, but the pellets they produce look more like Dots, the gum-drop candies … Go for it, if you're into that sort of thing! I'm not. Otherwise, if you're really curious to try pebble ice, the hack is to buy 10-pound bags of ice nuggets from Sonic (yes, the fast-food restaurant!) for around two dollars each (seriously!).

Otherwise, you can buy silicone molds for 1¼-inch cubes, 2-inch cubes, and spheres; ice picks and mallets; and a Lewis bag (a heavy canvas bag in which to crush ice) all at cocktailkingdom. com. If you don't want to buy a Lewis bag, you can DIY it with a kitchen towel and either

a rolling pin or the back of a heavy skillet. (You still need the feelings, though.)

Working ice just needs to be functional. And fresh.

I repeat: Make fresh ice if you want to enjoy a cocktail. That may mean planning in advance, but this is key! Ice will pick up the flavor of whatever aromas linger in your freezer, and you don't want your cocktail to taste like pasta sauce from last winter. So, inspect the landscape. If your freezer is jam-packed with food, make a new batch of ice. If you want to make drinks at home regularly, change out your ice every few days. If you're having a party, buy a few bags of ice from the grocery store and put them in a clean cooler. (You always need more ice than you think, anyway.)

Finally, as for the amount of ice in your shaker or mixing glass, you want enough to cover and then rise just above the wash line of the liquid.

A Few More Notes

On Mouthfeel

Mouthfeel means exactly what you think it does: It is the physical sensation(s) of a particular food or, in this case, drink, in your mouth. In short, mouthfeel is texture—creamy, bubbly, et cetera—and it's part of the overall taste experience.

Body belongs under the mouthfeel umbrella, but it has more to do with weight than texture. If something is full-bodied, it feels round, heavy, perhaps viscous. The complaint I hear most often about nonalcoholic mixed drinks is that they lack body, or they're "thin." (It's worth knowing that many distillers' dirty little secret is that they add glycerin to their spirits for better body.) There are ways around this: (1) Some ingredients, such as eggs, whey, and cream, are naturally weighty. (2) Sugar gives body to a drink, so much so that manufacturers of sugar-free beverages painstakingly play with hydrocolloids such as pectin, carrageenan, cellulose, and xanthan and gellan gums to reach the same effect. (3) Temperature affects viscosity. When a liquid is cold, it feels heavier on the palate.

All of that said, maybe we're doing these drinks a disservice by comparing them to cocktails. These don't have alcohol in them, and ethanol behaves in a particular way, so they're going to be different. And that's okay!

On Straws

Avoid plastic if you can. Buluh brand straws are made from bamboo, Aardvark makes paper straws that actually hold together, and Greens Steel metal straws are a good option, too.

On Inspiration

Once you've made some recipes from this book and start playing around on your own, here's how I want you to think about making good drinks: What are you trying to deliver? A flavor? A texture? A mood? A journey? Start there, then experiment and see what suits your tastes. And, speaking of that: Trust your own tastes!

The Drinks

But First, Syrup

Sugar doesn't dissolve in cold liquid, and honey is too thick to incorporate directly into cocktails, so you'll need to make syrups out of these sweeteners. Here are some basic recipes that are used throughout the book. (Recipes for any compound syrups, meaning those flavored with herbs or spices or the like, run with their corresponding drink recipes.)

Simple Syrup
MAKES 1¾ CUPS

In a small saucepan over medium heat, combine **1 cup water** and **1 cup granulated sugar**. Stir until the sugar dissolves, 3 to 5 minutes, then remove from the heat and let cool before using. Store in an airtight container in the refrigerator for up to 2 weeks.

Rich Simple Syrup
MAKES 1 CUP

In a small saucepan over medium heat, combine **½ cup water** and **1 cup granulated sugar**. Stir until the sugar dissolves, 3 to 5 minutes, then remove from the heat and let cool before using. Store in an airtight container in the refrigerator for up to 1 month.

Honey Syrup
MAKES 2 CUPS

Combine **1 cup mild honey** and **1 cup water** in a small saucepan over medium heat. Stir until the honey dissolves, 3 to 5 minutes, then remove from the heat and let cool before using. Store in an airtight container in the refrigerator for up to 2 weeks.

Rich Honey Syrup
MAKES 1½ CUPS

In a small saucepan over medium heat, combine **1 cup mild honey** and **½ cup water**. Stir until the honey dissolves, 3 to 5 minutes, then remove from the heat and let cool before using. Store in an airtight container in the refrigerator for up to 1 month.

Midday

Some of these drinks are caffeinated, some are sweet and creamy, some are bubbly and refreshing. All of them have a bright, sunny quality that places them—cheerfully!— in the morning or the middle of the day.

Billows & Thieves

MIKE DI TOTA — THE BONNIE, QUEENS, NEW YORK

Former Bonnie bar director Mike Di Tota's wife, Chelsea, doesn't drink, and this was her favorite cocktail on his menu. When I met her at the bar to try it out, I was skeptical: iced coffee and grapefruit juice? In a word: YES. Mike tried all the other citrus fruits in combination with coffee, but the bitter-on-bitter of grapefruit juice just worked. Make sure you shake *hard* to get that creamy froth on top.

COMMITMENT LEVEL ●○○○
SERVES 1

3   ounces freshly squeezed grapefruit juice
½   ounce freshly squeezed lemon juice
1   ounce cold-brew concentrate, such as Grady's
½   ounce Black Cardamom–Cinnamon Syrup (recipe follows)
Small pinch of smoked sea salt
Freshly grated nutmeg, for garnish

Combine the juices, cold-brew concentrate, syrup, and salt in a cocktail shaker. Fill with ice, seal the shaker, and shake vigorously for 20 seconds, until the shaker is ice cold. Double-strain into a coupe and finish with a grating of fresh nutmeg.

Black Cardamom–Cinnamon Syrup

MAKES ABOUT 1¼ CUPS, ENOUGH FOR 20 DRINKS

2   cinnamon sticks, cracked
3   black cardamom pods, cracked
½   cup water
1   cup maple syrup

In a small saucepan over medium heat, toast the cinnamon sticks, occasionally shaking the pan back and forth, until fragrant, 2 to 3 minutes. Add the cardamom, water, and maple syrup and simmer for 5 minutes. Remove from the heat and let cool completely. Fine-strain and discard the solids. Store the syrup in an airtight container in the refrigerator for up to 1 week.

Note Some additional and über scientific research I engaged in shows that leftover syrup can be used in your morning coffee.

Staycation

DANIEL MILLER — VEDGE, PHILADELPHIA, PENNSYLVANIA

Yuzu kosho is a Japanese fermented paste made with fresh chiles, salt, and yuzu citrus fruit. For this drink—and it really makes this drink—you want the green, not the red, variety. I love the heat it brings, so I increased the amount of yuzu kosho from Daniel's original recipe, but if you're not down with that, pull back on it a little. The condiment has grown in popularity in the States, so it may be sold at your local grocery store. If not, it's definitely at Japanese markets.

COMMITMENT LEVEL ●●○○
SERVES 1

1 ounce fresh pineapple juice
1 ounce freshly squeezed lime juice
1 ounce Pandan-Coconut Syrup (recipe follows)
½ teaspoon yuzu kosho
3–4 ounces soda water
1 cocktail umbrella, for garnish (optional)

Combine the juices, syrup, and yuzu kosho in a cocktail shaker. Fill with ice, seal the shaker, and shake for 10 to 15 seconds, until well chilled. Double-strain into a collins glass filled with ice and top with soda water. Garnish with a cocktail umbrella, if using, and serve.

Pandan-Coconut Syrup

MAKES 1½ CUPS, ENOUGH FOR 12 DRINKS

½ cup canned pandan leaves extract, such as Singing Bird
½ cup coconut milk
1 cup sugar

Combine the pandan extract, coconut milk, and sugar in a blender and blend on high for 1 minute. Store in an airtight container in the refrigerator for up to 1 week.

If making ahead and chilling, let the syrup stand at room temperature for 10 to 15 minutes, then shake to combine, if needed, before using.

Note Pandan is a tropical plant, its fragrant leaves often used in Southeast Asian cooking. Pandan extract is sold three ways: canned, as a paste, or as a concentrated extract. You want the milky stuff that comes in a can, called pandan leaves extract, for this recipe. While I can find it at most Thai grocers in New York City, some friends who live elsewhere (and who I let have early access to some of these recipes) had trouble finding it. If that's the case for you, Grocery Thai (grocerythai.com) sells it online. If you can't find it or don't want to mail-order, I also tested the Pandan-Coconut Syrup recipe with 1 full cup of coconut milk. It's a different drink—less vegetal, more like a spicy piña colada—but still delicious.

Jardín Verde

BRYAN DAYTON — CORRIDA, BOULDER, COLORADO

A former competitive trail runner who won two national championships, Bryan Dayton has offered nonalcoholic drinks at Oak at Fourteenth since the day he opened the Boulder restaurant more than ten years ago. My favorite, though, is this one from his fourth spot, Corrida. There are other recipes in this book that use Seedlip, but I think its best expression is like this, simply with tonic. The bubbles breathe life into all of those botanicals, and the sweet and bitter notes complement their flavors.

COMMITMENT LEVEL ●○○○
SERVES 1

1	cucumber ribbon for garnish
1½	ounces Seedlip Garden 108 (see page 29)
4	ounces Fever-Tree Mediterranean Tonic
1	sprig of fresh basil, for garnish

Line a wine or spritz glass with the cucumber ribbon and fill with 2 or 3 ice cubes. Add the Seedlip Garden 108 and tonic water. Garnish with the basil.

Batch for 6 Line 6 wine glasses each with 1 cucumber ribbon and set aside. (Or don't go to the trouble if you don't want to. It's beautiful, but, honestly, the drink is good either way!) Fill a pitcher with ice, then add 1 cup plus 2 tablespoons Seedlip Garden 108 and 3 cups Fever-Tree Mediterranean Tonic. Gently stir, then divide among the wine glasses. Garnish each with a basil sprig (again, only if you want to!).

Note You could use a regular tonic water, but Bryan likes Fever-Tree's Mediterranean Tonic because it's lighter on quinine and flavored with rosemary and lemon thyme. I'm with him.

Dollar Slice

AARON POLSKY — LISTEN BAR, NEW YORK, NEW YORK

Lorelei Bandrovschi is one of a few nightlife entrepreneurs providing New Yorkers with alcohol-free gathering spaces, and she tapped some of the best bartenders around the country to create drinks for Listen Bar, a pop-up series she launched in 2018. This riff on a Bloody Mary comes from Aaron Polsky, who's based in Los Angeles. He makes a next-level salt rim, bringing earthy and umami flavors from mushroom powder into the mix, but you could use a standard salt rim or Tajín Clásico chile-lime seasoning instead.

COMMITMENT LEVEL ●●●○
SERVES 1

Spiced Mushroom Salt
    (recipe follows)
1   lime wedge
2   ounces Seedlip Spice 94
    (see page 29)
4   ounces fresh tomato juice
1   teaspoon Tabasco
    Sriracha or other
    hot sauce
Small pinch of kosher salt
½   ounce freshly squeezed
    lime juice
1   sprig of oregano, for
    garnish
1   peperoncino, for garnish
    (optional)

Pour the mushroom salt into a small, shallow bowl. Rub the lime wedge around the rim of a large footed glass or collins glass. Dip the rim into the salt and set the glass aside.

    Combine the Seedlip Spice 94, tomato juice, Sriracha, salt, and lime juice in one half of a cocktail shaker and fill it halfway with ice. Dump the mixture into the other half of the shaker, then dump it back. Roll the drink this way two more times, so that it chills and aerates slightly without breaking ice or over-diluting. Pour it into the prepared glass and garnish with the oregano and the peperoncino, if using.

CONTINUED

Batch for 6 Pour the mushroom salt into a small, shallow bowl. Rub a lime wedge around each rim of 6 footed glasses. Dip the rim of each glass into the salt and set aside. Combine 1½ cups Seedlip Spice 94, 3 cups chilled tomato juice, 2 tablespoons hot sauce, 1 tablespoon kosher salt, and 3 ounces lime juice in a pitcher with ice. Stir until thoroughly combined, 10 to 15 seconds. Divide among the six prepared glasses, and garnish each with an oregano sprig and a peperoncino, if using.

Note I know I made a big fuss about using fresh tomato juice in the ingredients section (see page 26), but you can use store-bought if you really want to. If you go fresh, pureeing the tomatoes and fine-straining will get you the best results.

Dollar Slice
CONTINUED

Spiced Mushroom Salt
MAKES ¾ CUP, ENOUGH FOR
A HECK OF A LOT OF DRINKS

One 1-ounce packet dried
    shiitake mushrooms
3   tablespoons store-bought
    pizza seasoning
2   tablespoons hickory-
    smoked salt

In a spice grinder, blend the
shiitakes in three batches until
a powder forms. Transfer to a
bowl. Add the pizza seasoning
and salt to the grinder, then
blend until combined. Add to
the mushroom powder and stir
to combine. Store in an airtight
container at room temperature
for up to 2 months.

Chicha Morada Agua Fresca

ENRIQUE SANCHEZ — SCHOOL NIGHT, SAN FRANCISCO, CALIFORNIA

When he was growing up in Lima, Peru, Enrique Sanchez's family sold fruit and whenever a pineapple was about to go bad, into a pot of *chicha morada* it would go. "A batch of it was always sitting around," he says. The traditional Peruvian drink gets its color and texture from purple corn (Enrique likes the Inca's brand, which you can find at zocalofoods.com or amigofoods.com), and now Enrique serves it at School Night, where he's the beverage director. Here is his grandmother's recipe.

COMMITMENT LEVEL ●●●○
SERVES 1

5   ounces Chicha Morada (recipe follows)
¾   ounce freshly squeezed lime juice
¾   ounce Simple Syrup (page 37)
1   Granny Smith apple slice, for garnish

Combine the chicha morada, lime juice, and syrup in a tumbler filled with ice and stir. Garnish with the apple slice.

Chicha Morada
MAKES A SCANT 3 QUARTS, ENOUGH FOR 18 DRINKS

1   pineapple, washed and dried
1   pound whole dried purple corn (5 to 6 cobs)
1   Granny Smith apple, quartered
3   whole cloves
1   cinnamon stick
5   quarts plus ¾ cup water

Remove the top of the pineapple and discard. Cut the skin from the fruit, then core it, reserving the meat for another use (such as eating, maybe even as you prepare this drink!).

In a large stockpot, combine the pineapple skins and core with the corn, apple, cloves, cinnamon, and water. On the stovetop over high heat, bring the mixture to a boil. Decrease the heat to low and simmer for 2 hours, or until the liquid has reduced by an inch or two from the top and some kernels of the corn have split open slightly. Strain, discarding the solids, and let the liquid cool to room temperature, then refrigerate to chill. Store the chicha morada in an airtight container in the refrigerator for up to 1 week.

Batch for 6 Combine 3¾ cups Chicha Morada, a brimming ½ cup freshly squeezed lime juice, and ½ cup plus 1 tablespoon simple syrup in a pitcher. Stir, then divide among 6 tumblers filled with ice. Garnish each with an apple slice.

The Bicycle Gang

NICHOLAS MATIO — C3, BLOOMINGTON, INDIANA

I thought I'd do the bulk of my Indiana research in its capital, but it turns out that Bloomington, a little over an hour south of Indianapolis, is where it's really at for good drinking. (Even Cardinal Spirits—a distillery!—serves cold brew with mint syrup and chocolate bitters, or Golden Assam tea with passion fruit and club soda.) At C3, bar manager Nicholas Matio's riff on an Orange Julius is surprisingly simple with just four ingredients and two good shakes. It's a great brunch drink, if I do say so.

COMMITMENT LEVEL ●○○○
SERVES 1

3	ounces freshly squeezed orange juice
1	ounce heavy whipping cream
½	ounce Simple Syrup (page 37)
4–6	ounces soda water
1	orange twist, for garnish

Combine the juice, cream, and syrup in a cocktail shaker. Seal and shake vigorously for 10 seconds, until the cream has fluffed up and thickened. Open the shaker, fill with ice, then seal and shake for 5 to 8 seconds more, until well chilled. Strain into a large footed glass and top with soda water. Garnish with the orange twist.

Batch for 4 Most blenders can comfortably fit enough liquid for 4 servings. If your crowd is bigger than that, you can easily do two back-to-black blender rounds, no cleaning or fussing with the machine in between. Combine 1½ cups freshly squeezed orange juice, ½ cup heavy whipping cream, and ¼ cup simple syrup in a blender. Pulse 2 to 4 times, or until just combined. Add 2 to 3 ice cubes and blend just until the ice sounds broken up, 15 to 20 seconds. Divide between four footed glasses and top each with soda water. Garnish each with an orange twist.

Note Be patient when adding the soda water: Once the liquid gets close to the top of the glass, stop and wait for 20 seconds before pouring in the rest. The foam it creates should rise just above the rim.

Shiso Spritz

VICTOR GAINOR — VICIA, ST. LOUIS, MISSOURI

Shiso is in the mint family, so its season is mid–late summer. This drink's vaguely menthol, vaguely citrus flavor comes from a mixture of green and red (sometimes labeled as purple) shiso, both of which you should be able to find fresh at your local Asian grocers—but the recipe will work with just red shiso, too. At Vicia, the bar team mixes a syrup made from melon rinds into this drink, but the tonic adds enough sweetness for me. Use plain tonic water and a small squeeze of lemon juice (about ¼ teaspoon) if you can't find citrus tonic. The shiso tea is a light pinkish-brown before you add the citric acid and then, like *magic*, it becomes full-on magenta.

COMMITMENT LEVEL ●●○○
SERVES 1

2½ ounces chilled Shiso Tea
     (recipe follows)
2½ ounces citrus tonic,
     such as Fever-Tree
Shiso leaf, for garnish (optional)

Place 2 or 3 ice cubes in a wine glass. Add the tea, then the tonic water. Garnish with a shiso leaf, if using.

Shiso Tea

MAKES ABOUT 1¾ CUPS, ENOUGH FOR JUST OVER 4 DRINKS

1⅓ cups packed fresh
     red shiso leaves
⅔   cup packed fresh
     green shiso leaves
4   large fresh basil leaves
10   fresh mint leaves

Pour 2 cups water into a small saucepan and bring to a boil over medium-high heat. Add the red and green shiso leaves, the basil leaves, and the mint leaves, stir to submerge the herbs, decrease the heat, and gently simmer for 5 minutes. Strain the tea, pressing on the solids to extract as much liquid as possible. Discard the solids. Let the tea cool to room temperature, then chill thoroughly. Store in an airtight container in the refrigerator for up to 3 days.

Batch for 4 Fill a pitcher with ice. Add 1¼ cups tea and 1¼ cups tonic. Gently stir, then divide among 4 wine glasses filled with 2 or 3 ice cubes each. Garnish each with a shiso leaf, if using.

Honeydew-Avocado Agua Fresca

MEGAN SANCHEZ — GÜERO, PORTLAND, OREGON

Güero is, basically, a torta shop that also has a full cocktail bar featuring a selection of mezcals and tequilas. You'll find nonalcoholic beverages that are typical to Mexican restaurants—*horchata, agua de jamaica,* and Jarritos sodas—but co-owner Megan Sanchez takes extra care with her seasonal *aguas frescas.* Honeydew juice alone would have been fine in this drink, with some soda water and lime, but Megan adds avocado, turning it silky smooth.

COMMITMENT LEVEL ●●○○
SERVES 1

¾ ounce freshly squeezed lime juice
Pinch of kosher salt
3–4 ounces soda water, preferably Topo Chico
3 ounces Honeydew-Avocado Puree (recipe follows)
Tajín Clásico or other chile-lime seasoning powder, for garnish

Fill a collins glass with ice, then add the lime juice and salt. Add soda water, then top with the fruit puree. Gently stir to combine. Finish with a pinch of Tajín.

Honeydew-Avocado Puree

MAKES ABOUT 2½ CUPS, ENOUGH FOR JUST OVER 6 DRINKS

½ avocado, cubed
4 cups cubed honeydew

Combine the avocado, melon, and ¾ cup water in a blender and blend on high until smooth, about 1 minute. Fine-strain and discard the pulp. Store in an airtight container in the refrigerator for up to 3 days.

Note If you can't find Tajín, make your own chile-lime seasoning by mixing equal parts kosher salt, chile powder, and lime zest.

Espresso and Tonic with Lime

Food editor Rick Martinez on the drink that makes him feel like he's on vacation— even when he's at work in *Bon Appétit*'s offices.

It seemed very suspicious to me—I couldn't imagine drinking tonic in the morning—but a friend of mine who owns a café in Harlem called Shuteye fixed me one, and the only polite thing to do was to drink it. My mind was blown. It's transformative! The tonic turns a shot of espresso into something completely different, almost unrecognizable.

Normally, you see this drink with lemon, but because that's sharper, you have to be more judicious with it. Lime has tropical notes and a sweetness that I like. So I pull a long shot or, if I'm buying it, I order a double shot. I throw that into a pint glass filled with ice, top it with about 8 ounces of good-quality tonic, and squeeze a lime wedge into it. It's so balanced: The warm espresso melts the ice, which waters the coffee down a bit, and the tonic's sweetness with that bitter edge pulls out the tannins and the herbaceousness of the coffee, depending on what you're drinking. A dark

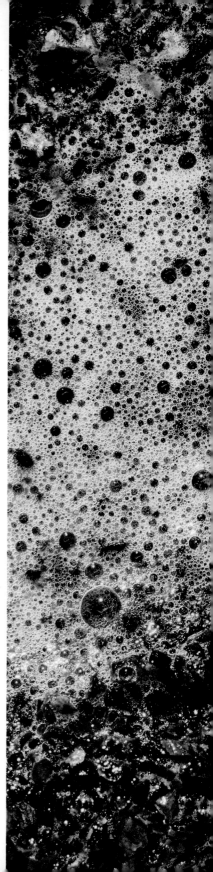

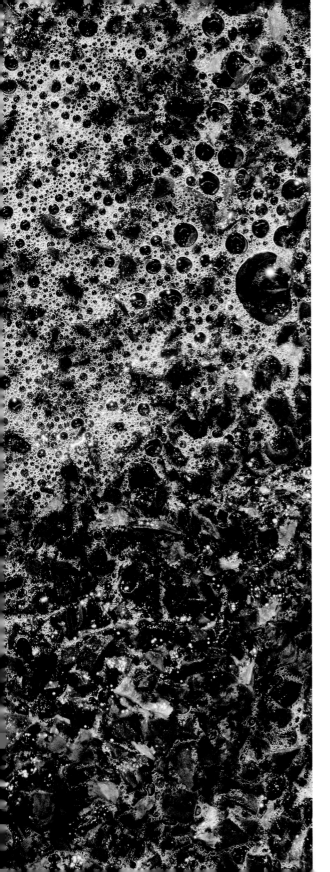

roast will clash with the tonic, so you want something lighter, with berry or stone fruit notes.

As much as I love a morning mug full of coffee, there's also a bit of monotony and drudgery associated with it for me, because it's usually the beginning of the workday. This feels like something that I should be enjoying on the beach.

Midnight Magic

Rick may like his espresso and tonic in the morning, but at Mission and Market, Eduardo Guzman pairs his version with dessert—preferably something rich and chocolaty. The Buckhead restaurant opened after my time in Atlanta—I was the food editor of *Atlanta* magazine for two very fun (and busy!) years—but I love the addition of bitters, which, with just one dash, usher this drink into the night.

●○○○ SERVES 1

7	ounces tonic water
1	ounce espresso
1	dash walnut bitters
1	lemon twist for garnish

Fill a collins glass with ice and pour in the tonic water. Top with the espresso and bitters. Garnish with the lemon twist.

Pimm's Crown

ROB BROUSE — ACADIA, CHICAGO, ILLINOIS

No one really knows *exactly* what Pimm's No. 1 is made of. The recipe for the gin-based liquor was developed centuries ago, and it's still a secret. What we *do* know is that it's delicious and worthy of replication. Rob Brouse's nonalcoholic version takes some work, but the pleasantly bitter, refreshing product is everything that's good about a Pimm's Cup. You could use all rooibos or all black tea, but I like the combination. The nonnegotiable: Whatever tea you use, it must be loose-leaf. A powder or the finer leaves in a sachet will make your drink too bitter.

COMMITMENT LEVEL ●●●●
SERVES 1

- 3 ounces "Pimm's" (recipe follows)
- ¼ ounce freshly squeezed lime juice
- 3 dashes of rhubarb bitters, such as Fee Brothers
- 3 ounces good-quality ginger ale, such as Goslings
- 1 sprig of mint, for garnish

Combine the "Pimm's," lime juice, and bitters in a cocktail shaker. Fill with ice, seal the shaker, and shake for 10 to 15 seconds, until well chilled. Double-strain into a footed glass and top with ginger ale. Garnish with the mint sprig.

"Pimm's"

MAKES 3 CUPS, ENOUGH FOR 8 DRINKS

- 2 oranges
- 2 lemons
- 2 limes
- ¾ cup sugar
- ¾ cup loose-leaf rooibos tea
- ⅓ cup loose-leaf black tea, such as Assam or English Breakfast
- 4 dried juniper berries
- 1 teaspoon gentian root
- 1¼ ounces raspberry vinegar
- 5 dashes of orange bitters
- 2 pinches of sea salt

Remove the peels from the oranges, lemons, and limes, leaving the white pith behind. Reserve the meat of the fruit for another use.

In a medium pot, combine the citrus peels with the sugar, teas, juniper berries, gentian root, vinegar, bitters, salt, and 3 cups water. Bring the mixture just to a simmer over medium-high heat. Remove the pot from the heat and let the ingredients steep for 1 hour. Transfer the mixture to an airtight container and chill in the refrigerator for at least 12 hours, or up to 24.

The next day, fine-strain the mixture and discard the solids. Store the "Pimm's" in an airtight container in the refrigerator for up to 1 week.

GOOD DRINKS

Note Purchase gentian root at mountainroseherbs.com.

Yu the Great

SAMANTHA AZAROW — DEPARTURE, PORTLAND, OREGON

Former beverage director Samantha Azarow leaned on coconut milk in order to keep Departure's menu dairy-free, and it works to marry two seemingly incompatible ingredients in this drink: basil and matcha. I tested the recipe with Italian basil, out of curiosity, and it didn't work. You really want Thai basil, which is less sweet, more herbal and licorice-like— spicy, even. It's grown domestically these days, and if it's not at your local supermarket, you can find it at Southeast Asian stores or order it online at importfood.com. Find matcha powder at most major grocery stores or at kettl.co. And feel free to bump up the lime juice to one ounce if you want more acidity.

COMMITMENT LEVEL ●○○○
SERVES 1

1   ounce Basil-Matcha Syrup
       (recipe follows)
¾   ounce freshly squeezed
       lime juice
1   ounce full-fat coconut
       milk, well shaken
3   ounces soda water
Matcha powder, for garnish

Combine the syrup, lime juice, and coconut milk in a cocktail shaker. Fill with ice, seal the shaker, and shake just to combine, about 3 seconds. Double-strain into a tumbler filled with ice and top with soda water. (This will produce foam, so pour slowly and carefully.) To garnish, sift matcha powder on top of the foam.

Basil-Matcha Syrup

MAKES 1¼ CUPS, ENOUGH FOR
10 DRINKS

1½   teaspoons matcha
       powder
1   cup loosely packed fresh
       Thai basil leaves
1   cup sugar

Combine the matcha powder, basil, sugar, and ¾ cup water in a blender and blend on high until smooth and bright green and the sugar is dissolved, about 2 minutes. Strain through a cheesecloth-lined strainer, discard the solids, and let the syrup cool to room temperature. The syrup will keep for 1 week in the refrigerator.

Batch for 6 Combine ¾ cup syrup, ½ cup plus 2 teaspoons lime juice, ¾ cup coconut milk, and 2 cups ice in a blender and pulse once or twice, just to combine. Divide among 6 tumblers and top each with soda water. Garnish each with a dusting of matcha powder.

Afternoon

It's late in the day and you've just come in from mowing the lawn. Or shoveling the sidewalk. Or swimming. Or you've been snug in a cozy chair, unable to move until you finish reading that book you love. These drinks will refresh you, soothe you, or pick you up when that late-afternoon slump hits.

U-Me & Everyone We Know

GABRIELLA MLYNARCZYK — AUTHOR OF *CLEAN AND DIRTY DRINKING*

As I wrote in the introduction, Gaby Mlynarczyk made a version of this drink for me in her Los Angeles kitchen. (She has since moved back east. Lucky me!) As I drove out of the city the next morning, my tongue watered as it re-registered the salinity of umeboshi vinegar and how it intensified the watermelon juice she had pressed. It was one of the first drinks I tasted during my trip that made me think, "We have a winner!" Gaby tends to lean on her pantry: coconut butter, pumpkin seed oil, and vanilla extract are just a few of the ingredients that find their way into her drinks. "I go bonkers for anything aromatic," she says. Me too.

COMMITMENT LEVEL ●●○○
SERVES 1

3   ounces Tomato-Watermelon Juice (recipe follows), well shaken
½   ounce freshly squeezed lemon juice
¾   teaspoon umeboshi vinegar
½   ounce Simple Syrup (page 37)
1   watermelon slice or 2 or 3 watermelon balls, for garnish

Combine the juices, vinegar, and simple syrup in a cocktail shaker. Fill with ice, seal the shaker, and shake just to combine, about 3 seconds. Double-strain into a tumbler filled with ice and garnish with a watermelon slice or watermelon balls.

Tomato-Watermelon Juice

MAKES 3 TO 4 CUPS, ENOUGH FOR 8-10 DRINKS

4½ cups cubed watermelon
2   medium heirloom tomatoes, quartered
3   cups loosely packed fresh basil leaves

Pass the watermelon, tomatoes, and basil through a juicer. Fine-strain the liquid into a container with a lid and discard the pulp. Cover and refrigerate the juice to chill thoroughly. (It will separate; this is okay. Just shake well before using.) Store in an airtight container in the refrigerator for up to 2 days.

Batch for 6 In a pitcher, stir 2¼ cups Tomato-Watermelon Juice, 3 ounces freshly squeezed lemon juice, 1½ tablespoons umeboshi vinegar, and 3 ounces simple syrup to combine. Refrigerate to chill thoroughly (the mixture will separate; this is okay). Just before serving, stir well to combine. Serve over ice and garnish each with a watermelon slice or balls.

Note You can find umeboshi vinegar, also called ume plum vinegar, at many major supermarkets (I like Eden brand), but ¼ to ½ teaspoon rice wine vinegar also works.

Nonalcoholic Beer Gets Good

Busch NA works as an ingredient in a mixed drink, but on its own, the texture is too flabby for me. Thankfully, a new generation of American craft breweries is fully focused on making better nonalcoholic beer in a variety of styles: Surreal Brewing, WellBeing Brewing, and, my favorite, Athletic Brewing Company.

Until these makers started playing around with technique, de-alcoholizing "normal" beer was the method of choice. Unfortunately, a lot of flavor is lost that way. Other methods include dilution, using newly discovered yeast strains that produce limited amounts of alcohol, and arrested fermentation. "None of them is perfect or easy," says Brooklyn Brewery's Garrett Oliver. (Brooklyn Brewery also makes an excellent hoppy nonalcoholic lager called Brooklyn Special Effects; check out brooklynbrewery.com.)

Athletic Brewing Company's lab is based in Stratford, Connecticut, where owner Bill Shufelt and brewer John Walker have settled on a process they won't reveal, other than to say that it's a convergence of a few methods and its patent is pending. "We brew a fully fermented beer to under 0.5% ABV, just controlling natural processes," says Shufelt. "We don't have to adulterate the product at the end." Whatever it is, it's working (especially when it comes to the IPA). Order at athleticbrewing.com.

Grapefruit Radler

JEFFREY MORGENTHALER — CLYDE COMMON, PORTLAND, OREGON

I've known Jeffrey Morgenthaler for quite some time now, and the way both of us drink has changed over the years. (Namely, we drink a lot less, if at all.) These days, Jeffrey's post-shift reward is a nonalcoholic Radler, typically a mixture of beer and something citrusy such as lemonade. As for the beer: "I have tried them all, and I can say the greatest nonalcoholic beer in America is Busch NA." Fighting words, but I won't fight with Jeffrey here. That's for the sidebar (opposite).

COMMITMENT LEVEL ●○○○
SERVES 1

1½   ounces freshly squeezed grapefruit juice
½   ounce freshly squeezed lemon juice
½   ounce Rich Simple Syrup (page 37)
1   ounce soda water
4–5 ounces nonalcoholic lager-style beer, such as Busch NA
1   lemon wedge, for garnish

Combine the juices, simple syrup, and soda water in a pint glass and fill with ice, then top with beer. Dump the mixture into either one half of a cocktail shaker or a fresh pint glass. Pour back into the first pint glass. Garnish with the lemon wedge.

Batch for 6 This works well as a pitcher drink. Rather, a two-pitcher drink, if you're serving 6 people. A standard pitcher holds 1 quart, and since this batched version makes about 1½ cups more than that, you'll need more than one vessel. Otherwise, just multiply the ingredients by 6 (1 cup plus 2 tablespoons grapefruit juice, 3 ounces lemon juice, 3 ounces rich simple syrup, ¾ cup chilled soda water, 3 cups nonalcoholic lager-style beer), combine them in pitchers with ice, and stir. Serve immediately.

Cherry, Ginger & Coconut Cream Ale

MELISSA AND FRAYSER MICOU — POMONA, RICHMOND, VIRGINIA

Pomona is the sweetest little café in Richmond's Union Hill, owned and operated by wife-and-husband team Melissa and Frayser Micou. They serve salads, toast with chutney—and some fun, soda shop-style drinks like this one. Choose a good-quality ginger beer with some bite to balance the sweetness. See "Dairy and Dairy-ish," page 27, for more information about buying and working with coconut cream.

COMMITMENT LEVEL ●○○○
SERVES 1

3 ounces ginger beer
4 ounces tart cherry juice
¼ cup Vanilla-Coconut Cream (recipe follows)

Fill a collins glass with ice, then add the ginger beer and cherry juice. Carefully spoon the coconut cream on top.

Vanilla-Coconut Cream

MAKES ABOUT 1½ CUPS, ENOUGH FOR 6 DRINKS

¼ cup sugar
½ teaspoon vanilla extract
¾ cup chilled coconut cream

In a small saucepan, combine the sugar, vanilla extract, and ¼ cup water and warm over medium heat, stirring until the sugar dissolves. Remove from the heat and let cool to room temperature. (You should have ⅓ cup syrup.) Store in an airtight container in the refrigerator for up to 1 week.

In a large mixing bowl, combine ¼ cup of the vanilla syrup (save the rest for another use, such as sweetening coffee) and the coconut cream. Whisk vigorously until the mixture thickens and gets frothy, like cold pancake batter (sounds weird, but that's what you want), about 2 minutes. (Well, it took my friend Mindy 2 minutes, but it took me 5. She's strong!) Use immediately.

Verjus Spritz

ADAM CHASE — CORVINO SUPPER CLUB, KANSAS CITY, MISSOURI

I hate to play favorites, but this is one of my go-to recipes because all it requires is the opening and pouring of three ingredients. Plus, I'm a sucker for the soft acidity of white verjus (buy Fusion brand at chefshop.com). Since I'm being opinionated here, now might be a good time to share that I *detest* thin, stringy lemon twists. This garnish has been manicured: It's peeled with a Y-peeler in order to get some real width, then trimmed on all sides, the top and bottom cut on a bias. *Très chic.*

COMMITMENT LEVEL ●○○○
SERVES 1

2   ounces white verjus
2   ounces soda water
2   ounces tonic water
1   lemon twist, for garnish

Combine the verjus, soda water, and tonic water in a wine or spritz glass filled with ice. Garnish with the lemon twist.

Batch for 6 Combine 1½ cups verjus, 1½ cups soda water, and 1½ cups tonic water in a pitcher filled with ice. Divide among 6 wine glasses and garnish each with a lemon twist.

Get Well Soon

JIM MEEHAN — AUTHOR OF *MEEHAN'S BARTENDER MANUAL*

Jim Meehan was my first-ever boss out of college. He is a legend in the bartending world, and I had the privilege of being his assistant on *Food & Wine*'s 2007 cocktail guide, a book of drink recipes the magazine used to publish annually. He's remained a supporter and a friend ever since, and now here I am, writing my own book, to which he so graciously contributed. Jim's drink is a toddy inspired by the Master Cleanse (!), and he calls it "a post snow-shoveling cocktail." If the flavor is too concentrated for you, simply add another ounce or two of hot water.

COMMITMENT LEVEL ●○○○
SERVES 1

¾ ounce freshly squeezed lemon juice
¾ ounce Turmeric-Ginger Honey Syrup (recipe follows)
1 tablespoon apple cider vinegar
Pinch of cayenne pepper
1 clove-studded lemon wheel, for garnish

Fill a mug with hot water and let it stand for 1 to 2 minutes to warm it.

Empty the mug and fill it with the lemon juice, syrup, vinegar, pepper, and 5 ounces hot water. Stir to combine. Garnish with the clove-studded lemon wheel.

Turmeric-Ginger Honey Syrup

MAKES JUST OVER ½ CUP, ENOUGH FOR 6 DRINKS

1 ounce fresh turmeric juice
1 ounce fresh ginger juice
⅓ cup honey

Whisk together the juices and honey until well combined. Store in an airtight container in the refrigerator for up to 1 week.

Batch for 6 Fill a 6- to 8-cup thermos with 3¾ cups hot water. Add ½ cup plus 1 tablespoon freshly squeezed lemon juice, ½ cup plus 1 tablespoon syrup, ¼ cup plus 2 tablespoons apple cider vinegar, and ¼ teaspoon cayenne pepper. Stir to combine, then divide among 6 pre-warmed mugs. Garnish each with a clove-studded lemon wheel.

The NYC Special

LAINEY COLLUM — PASS AND PROVISIONS, HOUSTON, TEXAS

Lainey Collum lives in San Francisco now, but she created this drink when she worked for the Pass and Provisions (which unfortunately closed in May 2019). For her, this drink represents the melting pot that is Houston: Vietnamese-style iced coffee inspired the use of sweetened, condensed milk; Mexican *café de olla* inspired the cinnamon; and, of course, there's good old American Coca-Cola.

COMMITMENT LEVEL ●○○○
SERVES 1

1 ounce Coffee Syrup (recipe follows)
1 ounce sweetened condensed milk
4 ounces Coca-Cola
1 whole star anise pod, for garnish (optional)

Combine the syrup and condensed milk in a cocktail shaker. Fill with ice, seal the shaker, and shake for 10 to 15 seconds, until well chilled. Double-strain into a collins glass filled with fresh ice, then top with the Coca-Cola. Gently stir with a barspoon to incorporate. To serve, float the star anise on the foam, if using.

Coffee Syrup

MAKES ¾ CUP, ENOUGH FOR 6 DRINKS

1 cinnamon stick
1 cup turbinado sugar
¼ cup medium-coarse ground coffee, preferably a fruity Ethiopian blend
¼ teaspoon vanilla extract
1 star anise pod

In a small saucepan, combine ¾ cup water with the cinnamon over medium heat and bring to a boil. Whisk in the sugar, coffee, and vanilla; turn the heat down to low; and gently simmer for 5 minutes.

Add the star anise, stir the mixture once, and remove from the heat. Let cool to room temperature, about 45 minutes. Then fine-strain the mixture, pressing on the solids to extract as much liquid as possible, and discard the solids. Store the syrup in an airtight container in the refrigerator for up to 2 weeks.

Batch for 6 You won't get the beautiful foam from this batch method that you do when using a shaker, but it still tastes, well, insane. In a bowl, whisk together ¾ cup syrup, ¾ cup sweetened condensed milk, and ¼ cup chilled water to combine. Divide the mixture among 6 collins glasses filled with ice, then top each with 4 ounces of Coca-Cola. Gently stir with a barspoon to incorporate. Garnish each with a star anise pod, if using, and serve immediately.

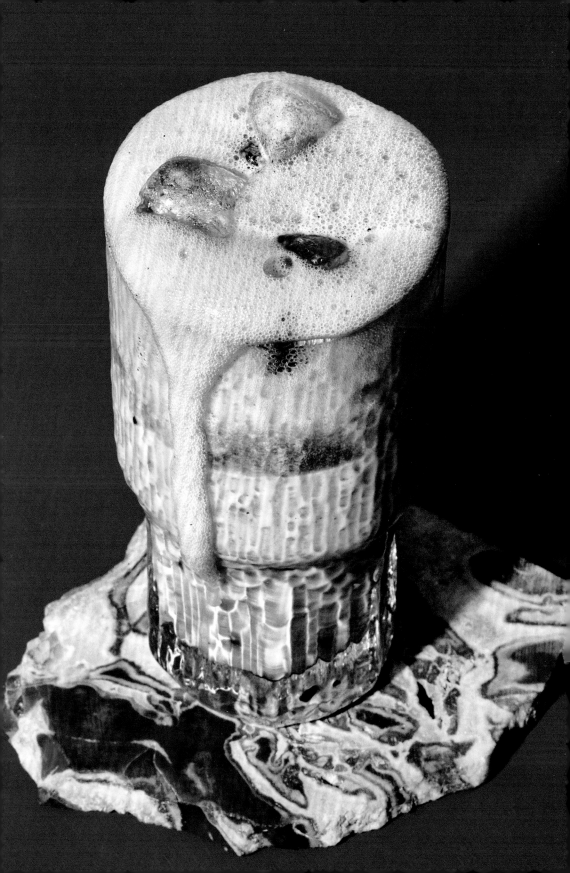

Tomato Water & Mint

MATTHEW KAMMERER — HARBOR HOUSE INN, ELK, CALIFORNIA

I was nervous to try my hand at a beverage developed by Matthew Kammerer, who won the restaurant at the Harbor House Inn a Michelin star in 2019. During our preliminary discussion, "dried celery root skin" and "burnt leaves" came up. Then he told me about some of the ingredients he grows on the northern California property: marigold, anise hyssop, salad burnett, cypress, alyssum . . . I gulped. But when he handed me this recipe, which originally called for yerba buena (I subbed in mint), I thought, "I can do that." And I did. And then I did again. And, even though I had to mail-order white soy sauce (food52.com), which, unlike regular soy sauce, won't overpower the drink, I will make it again—for a group of friends, since the Tomato Water only keeps for a day. The refreshing, vegetal flavor makes me think of that garden at the inn, even if I could never grow and maintain what's raised there. If your tomato is particularly sweet, level it out with more verjus or rice vinegar.

COMMITMENT LEVEL ●●○○
SERVES 1

3½ ounces Tomato Water
     (recipe follows)
1¾ ounces tonic water
White verjus and/or rice
     vinegar, as needed
1   sprig of mint, for garnish

Fill a tulip glass with crushed ice and add the tomato water. Top with the tonic water and gently stir. Adjust to taste with a little white verjus and/or rice vinegar, if needed. Garnish with the mint sprig.

Tomato Water

MAKES ABOUT 1 QUART, ENOUGH
FOR 9 DRINKS

2½ pounds ripe tomatoes,
     quartered
½   teaspoon sea salt
⅓   cup loosely packed fresh
     mint leaves
⅔   cup white verjus
1   tablespoon rice vinegar
1   tablespoon white or light
     soy sauce

In a blender, combine the tomatoes, salt, mint, verjus, vinegar, and soy sauce. Pulse a few times until the mixture resembles a salsa.

Transfer the mixture to a medium pot. Over high heat, bring it barely to a simmer, removing it from the heat after just 5 to 8 seconds. Line a strainer with 2 to 3 layers of cheesecloth and place the strainer over a bowl or large measuring cup. Strain the liquid into the bowl, wait 5 to 10 seconds, then set the strainer (still containing the solids) atop a clean container. Pour the already-strained liquid back over the solids in the strainer and let the liquid drip through until you have 3½ to 4 cups tomato water, about 45 minutes. The resulting liquid should be almost clear with a hint of gold. Discard the solids.

Refrigerate the tomato water until it's thoroughly chilled. Freshness of flavor declines quickly, so use it within 1 day.

Batch for 8 Fill 8 tulip glasses with crushed ice. Combine 3½ cups Tomato Water and 2 cups tonic water in a pitcher and gently stir. Adjust to taste with a little white verjus and/or rice vinegar, if needed. Divide among the 8 glasses and garnish each with 1 mint sprig.

Blackberry Cold Brew Colada

ANDERS LEHTO — HUDSON HILL, DENVER, COLORADO

This is such an easy, cheery coffee drink to serve for brunch, but it's also a great three p.m. pick-me-up treat. You just need one day of planning ahead to toss the fruit with the cold brew concentrate and let it work its magic. If you don't use it all up, the infused coffee keeps for two days and is delicious with just milk. (I've been known to prepare a six-person batch purely for myself, and while you don't need my permission to follow suit, I am still giving it. Enjoy yourself, you know?)

COMMITMENT LEVEL ●○○○
SERVES 1

3 ounces strained Blackberry-Infused Cold Brew (recipe follows)
1 ounce plain unsweetened almond milk
1 tablespoon coconut cream (see "Dairy and Dairy-ish," page 27)
1 orange twist, for garnish

Combine the cold brew, almond milk, and coconut cream in a cocktail shaker. Fill with ice, seal the shaker, and shake for 10 to 15 seconds, until well chilled. Double-strain into a rocks glass. Garnish with the orange twist.

Blackberry-Infused Cold Brew

MAKES 2¼ CUPS, ENOUGH FOR 6 DRINKS

2¼ cups blackberries
¾ cup thinly sliced navel orange
½ cup sugar
2¼ cups cold-brew coffee concentrate

Combine the blackberries, orange slices, and sugar in a medium bowl. Let sit at room temperature for 30 minutes. (This step is important! The sugar draws out the liquid from the fruit, and that's what will ultimately flavor the coffee.) Add the cold-brew coffee concentrate and stir to combine. Cover and chill in the refrigerator for 24 hours. Fine-strain and discard the fruit. Store in airtight container in the refrigerator for up to 2 days.

Note The coffee-soaked fruit is actually . . . really good. So, if you don't want to chuck it, reserve it in a separate container in the fridge after straining the cold brew. Toss a blackberry and an orange slice into the cocktail shaker when shaking your Colada, then pour it, without straining, into a rocks glass. The bitterness of the orange peel will have been tempered a bit, and the bits of blackberry pop in your mouth as you drink.

Lorca

PAM HANER — W.C. HARLAN, BALTIMORE, MARYLAND

"Smart drink!" my friend Adeena messaged after I posted this recipe on Instagram. Granted, Adeena lives in Tel Aviv and loves anything with tahini in it, but she was right: There's a smart balance going on here. The tahini is nutty; the kefir, or lightly fermented milk, lengthens the drink and balances the tahini with its sour notes; and the honey syrup rounds it all out with a slightly floral sweetness. I think of this (smart!) drink as a sophisticated milkshake.

COMMITMENT LEVEL ●○○○
SERVES 1

3   ounces plain kefir
1   ounce raw honey syrup
     (see method for Honey
     Syrup, page 37)
2   tablespoons tahini
1   sprig of mint, for garnish

Combine the kefir, honey syrup, and tahini in a cocktail shaker. Fill with ice, seal the shaker, and shake for 10 to 15 seconds, until well chilled. Double-strain into a tulip glass filled with crushed ice. Garnish with the mint sprig.

Batch for 6 Combine 1 cup plus 2 tablespoons kefir, ½ cup plus 1 tablespoon honey syrup, 3 ounces tahini, and 2 cups of ice in a blender and pulse once or twice, just to combine. Divide among 6 tulip glasses and garnish each with a mint sprig.

Limone e Sale

Bill Jensen, co-owner of
Tail Up Goat in Washington,
D.C., fell in love with what
he calls "the original electro-
lyte beverage" in Sicily.

 My wife and I
were traveling in
Italy before open-
ing Tail Up Goat,
and we stopped
in Catania, which
is in the shadow
of Mount Etna on the eastern side of Sicily. Everything
is made with black, volcanic
rock, and we were there in
August, so it was radiating
heat. Off of the central square,
you can find snack stalls and
soda fountains, where they
load up a glass with seltzer,
squeeze the lemon juice in
fresh, and then grab a mess
of sea salt with a barspoon
and stir it in.

   Like most professional
winos, I'm an acid freak, but
I'm also a salt freak. People
underestimate the importance
of salt, especially in drinks.

   We serve *limone e sale* at
the restaurant now: six ounces
of club soda, one ounce of
lemon juice, and a half teaspoon of flaky sea salt. Stirring
is hugely important, but I also
think part of the fun is testing
your tolerance: The drink gets
progressively saltier as you
move down. It's divisive, but
if one of our guests doesn't
like it, I'll just take
it off their check.
I'm not taking it
off the menu!

Nectar of the Gods

MINETTA GOULD — LADY JANE, DENVER, COLORADO

Brine and soda is a funkier, saltier, but equally simple alternative to syrup and soda. (Read Gyst fermentation center co-owner, Mel Guse, on the combination on page 101.) With this recipe, Minetta Gould kicks brine and soda up a notch, adding citrus juice to the mix and using jarred Sweety Drops, which are pickled Peruvian peppers. Peppadews, sweet cherry peppers, or even bread-and-butter pickles could work, too, but I recommend reducing or even omitting the simple syrup if you go the latter route.

COMMITMENT LEVEL ●○○○
SERVES 1

2 ounces freshly squeezed grapefruit juice
¾ ounce freshly squeezed lemon juice
½ ounce sweet pickle brine
½ ounce Simple Syrup (page 37)
5–6 ounces soda water
1 grapefruit slice or pickle, for garnish

Combine the juices, brine, and simple syrup in a collins glass and stir to combine. Add ice and top with soda water, gently stirring once more. Garnish with the grapefruit slice or pickle.

Batch for 6 Combine 1½ cups grapefruit juice, ½ cup plus 1 tablespoon lemon juice, 3 ounces brine, and 3 ounces simple syrup in a pitcher and stir to combine. Add ice and top with 3¾ cups soda water, gently stirring once more. Divide among 6 collins glasses, adding more soda water if you wish. Garnish each with a grapefruit slice or pickle.

Note You could keep a batch of the base (the juices, syrup, and brine) in the fridge for a couple weeks without losing much integrity. Just top with soda water to serve.

Don't Touch My Car Keys

SHELBY ALLISON — LOST LAKE, CHICAGO, ILLINOIS

The Pearl Diver is a classic Tiki glass, and when I look at it, I think sugar—especially if there's no alcohol to temper the sweetness of the juices and syrups that are part of the Tiki tradition. This drink, though, tastes more like coconut La Croix with bitters, except it has a silkier mouthfeel. You do need some special equipment: either a spindle drink mixer or a swizzle stick to aerate the liquid. I go for a full halo of bitters, meaning I soak the top of the ice until I see a shallow reddish-brown layer. Remember, though, that some bitters contain alcohol. See page 16 for other options.

COMMITMENT LEVEL ●●○○
SERVES 1

1½ ounces Coconut Syrup (recipe follows)
¾ ounce freshly squeezed lime juice
3 ounces soda water
5 dashes or more of aromatic bitters, such as Fee Brothers Old Fashioned Aromatic Bitters or Angostura
1 sprig of mint, for garnish

Fill a Pearl Diver or collins glass with crushed ice. Add the syrup, lime juice, and soda water. Using a single-spindle drink mixer, aerate the drink for 5 seconds. If you're using a swizzle stick, you'll need to work a little harder: Look for a frost to form on the glass, which should take around 20 seconds. (It all depends on how vigorously you swizzle.) Finish with the bitters and garnish with the mint sprig.

Coconut Syrup

MAKES ABOUT 2¾ CUPS, ENOUGH FOR 14 DRINKS

1 13½-ounce can unsweetened coconut milk
2 cups turbinado sugar

In a small saucepan, combine the coconut milk and sugar and set over medium-low heat. Whisk until the sugar dissolves and the mixture is smooth, about 5 minutes, then remove from the heat and let cool to room temperature.

Store in an airtight container in the refrigerator for up to 1 week. (It will separate; this is okay. Just shake well before using.)

The day's work is done! These celebratory or, in some cases, relaxing drinks are an occasion in and of themselves, helping you wind down and connect with friends.

King Palm

TYSON BUHLER — DEATH & CO, DENVER, COLORADO

This drink is *slick.* If you clarify the whey just right, it almost *glows.* Here's how: Buy a quart bottle of plain kefir, a lightly fermented milk, at the grocery store and strain it overnight through a fine-mesh strainer lined with eight layers of cheesecloth. You should end up with two cups of liquid—maybe less if some sediment settles at the bottom of the bowl and you need to pour the whey off of the top—which is more than enough for ten drinks. This liquid is what gives the drink some heft, but it's still light enough and has just enough acidity to wake up the palate before a meal. Be sure to buy clear, not pink, coconut water if you want your version to look like this one.

COMMITMENT LEVEL ●●●●
SERVES 1

1½ ounces kefir whey
1½ ounces coconut water
1   teaspoon Pineapple Syrup
     (recipe follows)
1   teaspoon Cinnamon Syrup
     (recipe follows)
1   grapefruit twist

Combine the whey, coconut water, and syrups in a mixing glass. Fill with ice and stir for 15 seconds, until well chilled. Strain into a chilled Nick & Nora glass. Squeeze the grapefruit twist over the top of the drink to express its oils, and discard.

Pineapple Syrup

MAKES ¾ CUP, ENOUGH FOR
36 DRINKS

½ cup fresh pineapple juice
½ cup sugar

In a blender, combine the pineapple juice and sugar and blend on high until the sugar has dissolved, about 2 minutes. Store in an airtight container in the refrigerator for up to 1 week.

Cinnamon Syrup

MAKES 1½ CUPS, ENOUGH FOR
72 DRINKS

4 cinnamon sticks
1 cup sugar

In a small saucepan, bring the cinnamon, sugar, and 1 cup water just to a boil and remove from the heat. Let stand for 15 minutes, then strain. Discard the solids. Store the syrup in an airtight container in the refrigerator for up to 1 week.

Batch for 6 Combine 9 ounces kefir whey, 9 ounces coconut water, 2 tablespoons pineapple syrup, 2 tablespoons cinnamon syrup, and 2 ounces cold water in a pitcher. Stir to combine.

Buckwheat Champagne

MICHAEL KUDRA — QUINCE, SAN FRANCISCO, CALIFORNIA

Save this for a special-occasion gathering; it's a sophisticated, celebratory drink that takes some prep work. (And you'll also have to source soy lecithin powder. Find it at modernistpantry.com or on Amazon.) The buckwheat tea tastes roasty-toasty and the oleo saccharum—a fancy word for the oil that's extracted when you mix citrus peels and sugar and let them sit around for a while—brightens it up. If you're using a SodaStream to carbonate, please do it in two batches. You want to be well below the fill line so that you get the optimum carbonation without overflow, which might damage your machine. (See "Carbonator," page 20, for more.)

COMMITMENT LEVEL ●●●●
SERVES 6

3   tablespoons buckwheat tea
3   cups just-boiled water
Small pinch of flaky sea salt
6   drops of Lemon Oleo Saccharum (recipe follows)
1½ ounces Simple Syrup (page 37)
6   teaspoons Lemon Air (recipe follows)

In a medium heatproof bowl, combine the tea and the water and let it sit for 2 to 3 minutes. Fine-strain the tea into another vessel and discard the solids. Add the salt and oleo saccharum to the tea and stir to combine. Let cool to room temperature, then refrigerate until chilled, about 2 hours or up to 4 days.

Just before serving, carbonate the tea mixture, then gently stir in the simple syrup. Pour into 6 champagne flutes and top each with about 1 teaspoon of Lemon Air.

Lemon Oleo Saccharum

MAKES ½ CUP, ENOUGH FOR MORE DRINKS THAN PEOPLE YOU KNOW

8   lemons
½   cup sugar

Remove the zests of the lemons in wide strips. (Y-shaped peeler only! See page 20.) Combine them with the sugar in a medium bowl and toss to coat, working the mixture with your fingers to press and bruise the peels. (Alternatively, you could use a muddler, if you have one, to bang them up a bit.) Cover and let sit at room temperature for at least 3 hours and up to 1 day. Fine-strain, pressing on the solids to extract as much oil as possible—this is liquid gold!—and discard the solids. Transfer the oil to a squeeze bottle with a small opening (you'll need this to measure in "drops" above). It will keep in an airtight container in the refrigerator for up to 1 week.

CONTINUED

Buckwheat Champagne

CONTINUED

Lemon Air

5   ounces freshly squeezed
    lemon juice
Scant ½ teaspoon soy lecithin
    powder

In a large, deep bowl combine
the lemon juice, soy lecithin
powder, and 1 tablespoon plus
2 teaspoons room-temperature
water. Using an immersion
blender, blend the mixture
with the blade at a 45-degree
angle until most of the liquid
has turned into foam, 20 to
30 seconds. (If you don't have
an immersion blender, you can
use a blender, hand mixer, a
whisk, or even a cocktail shaker
if you shake it vigorously. You're
just trying to incorporate air
in there!) Let the foam sit for a
minute before using; this will
ensure that it keeps its shape
and is easily spoonable. Use
immediately after that.

Note Roasted buckwheat tea might be labeled as *soba-cha* (Japanese), *memil-cha*
(Korean), or *ku qiao cha* (Chinese), and note that there are subtle flavor differences
country to country. If you can't find it at your local Asian grocer, buy it online at Harney
& Sons (harney.com).

More on Oils

Essential oils can help you push a drink in a completely unexpected direction. They allow you to access a vast range of flavors—sandalwood, rosewood, jasmine—that are hard to come by otherwise.

When I say flavor, by the way, I mean taste plus smell. "Taste is just what the taste buds tell you: sweet, salty, bitter, sour, or umami," says Kevin Peterson, co-owner of Sfumato Fragrances in Detroit, Michigan. Much of the nuance of flavor, he says, happens when molecules in foods or drinks enter the nasal passages through the mouth, a process called retro-nasal olfaction. "Flavor is defined as whatever is hitting your tongue plus whatever is going up your nose."

By day, Sfumato may be a perfume shop where Kevin and his wife Jane sell a range of homemade fragrances, but by night, the space becomes Castalia, a cocktail bar with a menu based on those scents. Your drink arrives at the table with a napkin that's been spritzed with a corresponding perfume; the idea is to take a sniff for every sip. Before you start experimenting with fragrant essential oils at home, though, Kevin says it's important to know a few things: (1) Not all essential oils are food-safe. Look for "GRAS" (Generally Recognized as Safe), "FDA Approved for Food Use," or "FDA Approved for Internal Use" on the label. If none of those is listed, it's a no-go. ("Organic" does not mean "approved for food use," either.) (2) Because essential oils are so highly concentrated, getting the proper amount into a drink can be tricky. "One drop is enough to completely overpower a cocktail," Kevin says. The fix is to dilute the oil in simple syrup—we're talking about starting with as little as 1 drop per 16 ounces of syrup, then adding more if needed. (3) The more unusual essential oils tend to be the more expensive ones, but remember, they're often sold by the half ounce. Used by the drop, that half ounce will last you quite a long time. (There are several hundred drops in a half ounce.)

Here are some of Kevin's favorite flavor combinations:

Oil: balsam of Peru
Characteristics: vanilla, sugar cookie
Works with: warm drinks; sweet drinks like hot chocolate

Oil: clary sage
Characteristics: bright, sharp
Works with: citrus drinks; enhances their brightness

Oil: juniper
Characteristics: woody, piney, gin-like
Works with: carbonated beverages

Oil: jasmine
Characteristics: floral, musky
Works with: tea-based beverages

Salted Rosemary Paloma

NAREN YOUNG — DANTE, NEW YORK, NEW YORK

For a fairly simple drink, this tequila-less Paloma has real depth of flavor. Pungent rosemary pairs well with grapefruit, and I like that the salt gets mixed into the syrup instead of stuck on the glass's rim, so it disperses throughout the drink. This is the kind of bitter, punchy, refreshing cocktail I want in my hand while the sun goes down.

COMMITMENT LEVEL ●●○○
SERVES 1

½ ounce Salted Rosemary Syrup (recipe follows)
2–3 ounces freshly squeezed grapefruit juice
½ ounce freshly squeezed lime juice
3 ounces soda water
1 grapefruit slice, for garnish

Fill a collins glass with ice. Add the syrup and juice, then top with soda water and gently stir. Garnish with a grapefruit slice.

Salted Rosemary Syrup

MAKES ABOUT ½ CUP, ENOUGH FOR 8 DRINKS

3 tablespoons sugar
1 teaspoon Maldon sea salt
1 sprig of rosemary, cut crosswise into 3 pieces

In a small saucepan, combine the sugar, salt, rosemary, and 3 ounces water and warm over medium heat, stirring until the sugar is dissolved. Remove from the heat and let cool to room temperature, then fine-strain and discard the solids. Store the syrup in an airtight container in the refrigerator for up to 1 week.

I'VE BEEN DRINKING

Brine and Soda

Mel Guse, co-owner of
Gyst fermentation center in
Minneapolis, Minnesota, loves
wine and beer, but she *loves*
brine with soda.

 Sauerkraut brine, to be specific. Our sauerkraut at Gyst is super simple: It's just salt and cabbage, and we let that ferment for three weeks.

The way I make the drink, it's almost like a nonalcoholic margarita: I salt the glass, fill it with ice, then add one and a half ounces of brine, top it with soda water, and squeeze half a lime on top. For me, it's almost like a savory aperitif. It gets the palate going, with the acidity and salt and bubbles, so I drink it before eating a fuller meal.

At home, you could use the brine from whatever pickles are in your fridge, just know that you'll get different outcomes. Kimchi is a little funkier and spicier. Fermented beets are earthier and will give the drink a more viscous quality. Bread-and-butter pickles work if you like sweetness. Whatever you choose, I recommend lacto-fermented brines, which have the good bacteria in them that our body craves. There's something in there that makes us feel alive!

Shimeji Mushroom Elixir

KATIE RUE — RECEPTION BAR, NEW YORK, NEW YORK

Reception Bar owner Katie Rue serves cocktails and Korean snacks such as *dukbokki* and *japchae mandu* in a bright lounge (not an oxymoron in this case!) on New York's Lower East Side. The combination of quince honey and mushrooms in this drink is meant to improve blood sugar and boost the metabolism, but I'm all in for the savory shrub and the toasty flavor of the buckwheat tea. (Find quince honey in the tea aisle of most Asian, especially Korean, grocers.) Katie garnishes her version with tart yumberry powder, but freeze-dried strawberries are more readily available. I got mine at Trader Joe's. If it's humid out, use the powder immediately.

COMMITMENT LEVEL ●●●○
SERVES 1

1 ounce Shimeji Mushroom Shrub (recipe follows)
½ teaspoon quince honey (optional)
5 ounces chilled carbonated Buckwheat Tea (page 104)
Freeze-dried strawberries, pulverized in a spice grinder, for garnish (optional)

Combine the shrub and honey, if using, in a collins glass and stir. Fill with ice, then top with the tea. Gently stir once more, then dust the top of the ice with strawberry powder, if using.

Shimeji Mushroom Shrub

MAKES ABOUT 1¼ CUPS, ENOUGH FOR 10 DRINKS

1 pound white or brown Shimeji (also known as Beech) mushrooms, washed and trimmed
1 cup distilled white vinegar
1 cup sugar
¼ teaspoon kosher salt

In a medium saucepan, combine the mushrooms, vinegar, sugar, and salt over medium-high heat. The mushrooms may not be covered by the liquid, but this will change as the mixture cooks. Bring to a boil, stirring here and there to coat all of the mushrooms and to help them cook down, and then decrease the heat to low. Gently simmer for 15 minutes. Remove from the heat, let cool, then strain. Discard the solids. Let the shrub "marinate" for at least 24 hours in an airtight container in the refrigerator before using. Store in the refrigerator for up to 1 month.

CONTINUED

Shimeji Mushroom Elixir

CONTINUED

Buckwheat Tea

Roasted buckwheat tea might be labeled as *soba-cha* (Japanese), *memil-cha* (Korean), or *ku qiao cha* (Chinese), and there are subtle flavor differences country to country. If you can't find it at your local Asian grocer, buy it online at Harney & Sons (harney.com).

Buckwheat soaks up more liquid than you might be used to seeing with tea, so I'm including brewing instructions to get you the 5 ounces you'll need (with a little wiggle room). Steep 1 tablespoon tea in 7 ounces just-boiled water for 5 minutes, uncovered. This should get you 6 ounces of tea; I recommend brewing a tiny bit more than you need because it's tricky to get exact amounts with this tea. It's thirsty stuff! Strain and let cool to room temperature, then refrigerate until chilled. Just before serving, carbonate the tea.

Batch for 6 Combine ¾ cup shrub and 1 tablespoon honey, if using, in a pitcher and stir well to combine. Fill the pitcher with ice and top with 3¾ cups carbonated tea. (The ratio for this amount of tea: Pour 4½ cups boiling water over ¼ cup plus 2 tablespoons buckwheat tea. Steep, uncovered, for 5 minutes, and you should have 4 cups of tea. Be sure to carbonate in batches, as this is a large volume.) Gently stir, then divide among 6 collins glasses. Garnish each with a dusting of strawberry powder, if using.

Note Shimeji mushrooms, which are sold at Asian markets, farmers' markets, or specialty grocers, come connected to a kind of "pad" of roots. To free them, just cut close to their bottoms. And yes, they do naturally have a funky odor, so if you're in your kitchen right now, inspecting and sniffing, rest assured. Everything is as it should be!

Pear Cider

SINGLETHREAD — HEALDSBURG, CALIFORNIA

When you walk into SingleThread, you'll find yourself in a small vestibule, facing a window into the kitchen. One of the restaurant's chefs will slide open that window and hand you a drink—always nonalcoholic—made from seasonal ingredients grown on SingleThread's farm just seven miles away. This pear cider is one of those "welcome drinks," as head chef and co-owner Kyle Connaughton calls them. I've taken liberties with the recipe to make it as home-cook friendly as possible, but the surprise element is still intact: By the watery look of the clarified juice, you simply can't anticipate the intensity of flavor.

COMMITMENT LEVEL ●●●●
SERVES 6

5	very ripe Bosc pears
1	tablespoon freshly squeezed lime juice
½	vanilla bean, split in half lengthwise
1½	teaspoons agar

Fill a large (really large!) bowl with ice and set aside.

Peel, core, and cube the pears, tossing the pieces in a bowl with the lime juice as you go to preserve their color. (They will, inevitably, turn at least beige but the acid will help slow the process.) Transfer to a blender and blend on high until smooth.

Meanwhile, scrape the seeds from the vanilla bean. In a medium saucepan, combine them with the vanilla bean pod and 3 cups water and bring to a boil. Add the agar and whisk constantly, to activate it, for 4 minutes. Remove from the heat.

Working quickly, transfer the pear puree to a medium bowl and set it inside the larger bowl with ice. Add the hot vanilla-water mixture in a slow stream, whisking as you go. Continue to whisk the mixture until it has come down to room temperature or just below, about 4 more minutes.

Leave the mixture in the ice bath, being careful that no melted ice flows in, until it sets up and is almost the consistency of Jell-O, 1 to 2 hours. Transfer the mixture to a fine-meshed sieve lined with four layers of cheesecloth and strain the juice into a large bowl. This will take a couple of hours, if not more. The liquid should be clarified, meaning that it's see-through if not colorless (mine was the color of chamomile tea). If at first some cloudiness comes through, let it drip until the liquid runs transparent, then pour the cloudy liquid back into the strainer so that it all ultimately runs clean. Discard the solids. Store the cider in an airtight container in the refrigerator for up to 1 day.

Divide among 6 chilled coupe glasses and serve.

Don't Call Me Shirley

WILL STEWART — COLTIVARE, HOUSTON, TEXAS

This drink asks *not* to be called Shirley. It is far from a Shirley Temple—respect it! Three ingredients help usher it into adulthood: Saba, a cousin of balsamic vinegar (actually the first step in the balsamic-making process) brings a raisiny quality; sherry vinegar wakes up the mix with its punchy acidity; and a little bit of syrup from a jar of Luxardo cherries adds sweetness but also depth. Speaking of a little bit: At just over 2 ounces, this is a short drink, but, given the multiple syrups and sharp acids, a little goes a long way.

COMMITMENT LEVEL ●○○○
SERVES 1

½	ounce Luxardo cherry syrup
¼	ounce saba
½	teaspoon sherry vinegar
½	ounce freshly squeezed lemon juice
¾	ounce freshly squeezed orange juice
1	Luxardo cherry, for garnish
1	orange slice, for garnish
1	sprig of mint, for garnish

Combine the syrup, saba, vinegar, juices, and ¾ teaspoon water in a cocktail shaker. Fill with ice, seal the shaker, and shake for 30 seconds, until well chilled and a foam has formed. Double-strain into a tulip glass filled with crushed ice. Garnish with the cherry, orange, and mint sprig.

Note Find saba at gustiamo.com and Luxardo cherries at specialty stores or at snukfoods.com.

Fizzy Hop Tea

CHARLES BABINSKI — GO GET EM TIGER, LOS ANGELES, CALIFORNIA

When you crack an end-of-workday beer, what are you really after? For some, it's the alcohol, but for me—and for Go Get Em Tiger co-owner Charles Babinski—it's the bitter bite of hops. Make sure to use whole cone hops instead of the pellet version, which would be too strong and would also produce sediment. Find the dried Citra leaf hops at Northern Brewer (northernbrewer.com). As for the tea, I used Song Tea's Old Tree Yunnan Red (songtea.com).

COMMITMENT LEVEL ●●○○
SERVES 3

2   tablespoons Yunnan red tea leaves
1   heaping tablespoon whole cone Citra hops
5   teaspoons Simple Syrup (page 37)

In a glass or plastic container with a lid, combine the tea and hops with 3 cups cold water. Cover and let sit in the refrigerator for at least 24 hours, or up to 2 days. Strain, discarding the hops and tea. Carbonate, then gently stir in the simple syrup.

Note Remember! It's important to wait until your drinks are carbonated before sweetening them. The more sugar in your liquid, the less space there is for gas, and that surface tension will create foam. See "Carbonator," page 20, for more.

Apple & Miso

SEAN UMSTEAD — KINGFISHER, DURHAM, NORTH CAROLINA

Dark, complex, and savory, this drinks almost like a scotch on the rocks. Sean Umstead juices Pink Lady or Honeycrisp apples at his bar, but he says that store-bought apple juice is a fine substitute. (I urge you to go fresh! Sorry to complicate things!) He bumps up the acidity without overpowering the apple by mixing in some citric acid. "Once you start to add lemon juice, it tastes like a traditional sour," says Umstead. "You lose that apple-y nuance." Find citric acid at nowfoods.com or modernistpantry.com.

COMMITMENT LEVEL ●●○○
SERVES 1

½   cup apple juice
2   tablespoons Miso Syrup (recipe follows)
⅛   teaspoon citric acid
1   fresh shiso leaf, for garnish

Combine the apple juice, syrup, and citric acid in a cocktail shaker. Fill with ice, seal the shaker, and shake for 10 to 15 seconds, until well chilled. Double-strain into an old-fashioned glass filled with ice. Garnish with the shiso leaf.

Miso Syrup

MAKES ABOUT ¾ CUP, ENOUGH FOR 6 DRINKS

1   vanilla bean
¼   cup packed fresh shiso leaves
½   cup sugar
½   cup just-boiled water
¼   cup red miso

Scrape the seeds from inside the vanilla bean and put them in a blender. Add the shiso leaves, sugar, and water to the blender and blend for 1 minute. Add the miso and blend for another 30 seconds. Strain through a cheesecloth-lined strainer, discard the solids, and let the syrup cool. Store in an airtight container in the refrigerator for up to 3 days.

Batch for 6 Combine 3 cups fresh apple juice, ¾ cup syrup, ¾ teaspoon citric acid, and 2 cups of ice in a blender and pulse once or twice, just to combine. Fine-strain among 6 rocks glasses filled with fresh ice. Garnish each with 1 shiso leaf.

Note Any extra miso syrup would work with pork or drizzled over a bowl of vanilla ice cream. Just saying.

Sanbitter

Josh Harris, co-owner of Trick Dog and Bon Voyage in San Francisco, California, doesn't think of San Pellegrino's Sanbitter as a soda. (He wouldn't hide soda from his friends.)

 It drinks more like Campari than anything else—it's aperitif-like in viscosity and it hits all the parts of your tongue that I'm chasing when I put together a cocktail—which means that I either drink it on the rocks or I add something effervescent to it.

Fever-Tree's bitter lemon tonic is dry, so it plays nicely with the sweetness in Sanbitter. You could put San Pellegrino's Limonata with it, but then it's going to drink more like a soda. With tonic, it drinks more like a cocktail. Sometimes I just mix it with sparkling mineral water, but it has to have a big bubble, like Topo Chico.

Because Sanbitter isn't readily available in the United States, I savor it. I'll drink one after I've had a hard day of work or when my wife is having a glass of wine and, to be honest, I put them away when I have friends over. It's like when you have a really nice bottle of whiskey: When company calls, you put the Pappy Van Winkle in the cabinet and offer Wild Turkey!

More Bitter Sodas to Try

Sanbitter—Jolly Rancher-red in color, just like Campari—is only the beginning. Italy has a long-standing love of bitter sodas, and while we still have to know an Italian grocer or poke around online to get hold of a ten-pack, the United States is starting to catch on.

Made in Italy

Sanbitter Dry San Pellegrino also makes a clear version of Sanbitter. It's packed in those same 3½-ounce bottles, but it has a drier, gentian-root bitterness to it.

Chinotto A number of companies make soda from *chinotto*, a bitter orange that's found all over Italy. My favorites are San Pellegrino Chinotto and Italian brewer Baladin's Spuma Nera.

Stappj Red Bitter Stappj makes a *chinotto* as well as eight other soda flavors. The best is its red bitter, which is very similar to Sanbitter in sweetness, bitterness, viscosity, and color.

Crodino Originally made in Crodo, in Italy's Piedmont region, Crodino was bought by Gruppo Campari in the 1990s. It's pale orange in color (called a "blonde" *aperitivo*, or pre-dinner drink), and tastes of bitter orange, cardamom, and vanilla.

Biz I've never gotten my hands on Biz, but there are three flavors: the golden bitter is made with Sicilian citrus, and both the red and the white get their bitterness from aromatic herbs and ginseng extract.

Martelli Bitter Rosso and Oro I've had no luck finding Martelli's bitter sodas in the States; the generous photographer (and former pastry chef) Nikole Herriott smuggled some in from Canada for me. (Thanks, Nikole!) Both the Rosso (red) and the Oro (gold) are slightly less viscous than Sanbitter, and I like the former on its own or with orange juice.

Made in America

Top Note Tonic Based in Milwaukee, Wisconsin, former craft brewer Mary Pellettieri makes a line of sodas and syrups including bitter lemon soda, an Indian tonic that she calls "the IPA of tonic water," a gentian tonic syrup, and a bitter orange syrup.

Bitter Love The women behind this Portland, Maine, company call Bitter Love "sparkling drinking bitters." The best flavor, in my opinion, is the peppered grapefruit, which gets its bitterness from a blend of ashwagandha, gentian, ginger, artichoke, and artemisia annua.

Casamara Club These "amaro soft drinks" are made in Detroit, Michigan, with *chinotto*. More herbal than bitter in flavor, they come in four flavors: Alta, which mimics a lighter, drier Negroni; lemon- and sage-infused Onda; Capo, made with chamomile and licorice; and Sera, kind of like a cinnamon-y Aperol spritz.

Like My Father

HUNTER DOUGLAS — HANK'S COCKTAIL BAR, WASHINGTON, D.C.

Hunter Douglas's original title for this drink was Like My Father, an Old-Fashioned Teetotaler, which is . . . a lot to say. I've shortened it, but I want to point out that this is Hunter's riff on an old-fashioned, which contains bourbon or rye, sugar, water, and bitters (and that's why it was in the name). Soda made with *chinotto*, a bitter orange that's found all over Italy, is good on its own, but combined with the DIY tea bitters in this drink it really leans into its bitter side. In my opinion (and Hunter's) that makes it even better.

COMMITMENT LEVEL ●●○○
SERVES 1

5   ounces chinotto soda, such as San Pellegrino
1   teaspoon Tea Bitters (recipe follows)
1   orange twist, for garnish

In a rocks glass filled with one large ice cube, combine the chinotto and bitters. Squeeze the orange twist over the drink to express its oils, and drop it into the glass.

Tea Bitters

MAKES ABOUT 1/3 CUP, ENOUGH FOR 16 DRINKS

2   teaspoons loose-leaf black tea
1   cup just-boiled water

Combine the tea with the water in a small heatproof bowl and cover. Let steep for 4 hours (no, that is not a typo!), then fine-strain the tea into a small saucepan and discard the solids.

Bring the brewed tea to a boil over high heat. Decrease the heat to low and simmer until the liquid is reduced to 3 ounces, about 10 minutes. Remove from the heat and let cool completely. Tea bitters can be made ahead and kept chilled for up to 1 month. (Chilled tea bitters will turn a little cloudy; this is okay.)

Batch for 6 Combine 3¾ cups chinotto and 1½ tablespoons bitters in a pitcher and gently stir. Divide the liquid among 6 rocks glasses, each filled with one large ice cube, and garnish each with an orange twist. Serve immediately.

Padova Spritz

TOBIN SHEA — REDBIRD, LOS ANGELES, CALIFORNIA

It's five o'clock on a summer Friday. This is the drink for that. Serve it with a bowl of potato chips (Utz, please) and another little bowl of extra olives and sit outside with a friend. That's all I have to say about that!

COMMITMENT LEVEL ●○○○
SERVES 1

2	ounces chinotto soda
1½	ounces red verjus
1	ounce soda water
1	orange twist, for garnish
1	green pitted olive, for garnish

Fill a spritz or wine glass with 2 or 3 ice cubes. Add the chinotto, red verjus, and soda water. Garnish with the orange twist and olive.

Batch for 6 Fill a pitcher with ice. Add 1½ cups chinotto, 1 cup plus 2 tablespoons verjus, and ¾ cup soda water. Gently stir, then divide among 6 wine glasses. Garnish each with an orange slice and an olive.

Sunomono

SEAN UMSTEAD — KINGFISHER, DURHAM, NORTH CAROLINA

For Sean Umstead, cocktails and food are no different: "This drink is composed, like a dish," he says. The elements here are light, refreshing cucumber juice balanced by rice vinegar infused with sesame, which gives it depth. Salt brings everything together. To make a cucumber ribbon garnish, use a Y-shaped vegetable peeler and slice the cucumber lengthwise. It should stick to the glass if you gently press the ribbon into it.

COMMITMENT LEVEL ●●○○
SERVES 1

1   cucumber ribbon, for garnish
3   ounces fresh cucumber juice
1   ounce Sesame and Salted Rice Vinegar Shrub (recipe follows)
4–5 ounces soda water

Line a collins glass with the cucumber ribbon. Add the juice and shrub, fill the glass with ice, and stir to combine. Top with soda water.

Sesame and Salted Rice Vinegar Shrub

MAKES 1½ CUPS, ENOUGH FOR 12 DRINKS

1   teaspoon sesame seeds
1¼ cups rice vinegar
¼   teaspoon kosher salt
¾   cup sugar

Toast the sesame seeds in a small sauté pan over medium heat, stirring frequently, until fragrant, about 1 minute. In a small saucepan over medium heat, combine the toasted sesame seeds and the vinegar, then add the salt and sugar. Stir constantly, until the sugar is dissolved, about 1 minute. Remove from the heat.

Transfer the mixture to a blender and blend on high until smooth, about 30 seconds. Let sit for 30 minutes so that the flavors mingle, then fine-strain and discard the solids. Store the shrub in an airtight container in the refrigerator for up to 1 month. (It will separate; this is okay. Just shake well before using.)

Batch for 6 Line 6 collins glasses each with one cucumber ribbon and set aside. Combine 2¼ cups cucumber juice, ¾ cup shrub, and 3 cups soda water in a pitcher filled with ice and give the mixture a gentle stir. Divide among the collins glasses, adding more soda water if you wish.

Evening

These drinks are meant to be paired with food, so they use certain fruits and vinegars for their acidic qualities and tea for tannic ones. If you are (or were!) more of a beer person, there is finally an array of good nonalcoholic beers to choose from (see page 68).

Squash & Sorghum

BRAD LANGDON — THE DABNEY, WASHINGTON, D.C.

The main cooking method at the Dabney? Live fire. (The hearth was constructed by chef-owner Jeremiah Langhorne's father and brother.) Inevitably, roasted fruits and vegetables find their ways into beverage director Brad Langdon's cocktails, but in the case of this butternut squash shrub, it's the squash *juice* that gets cooked. This step takes a raw, almost potato-y liquid and turns it into something rich and toasty with a beautifully rusty color. Paired with a watercress salad or roasted pork, this makes for a great fall meal.

COMMITMENT LEVEL ●●●○
SERVES 1

1½ ounces Squash and Sorghum Shrub (recipe follows)
4 ounces soda water

Place one large ice cube in a rocks glass. Pour in the shrub, then top with the soda water.

Squash and Sorghum Shrub

MAKES 1½ CUPS, ENOUGH FOR 8 DRINKS

1 butternut squash, peeled, seeded, and cut into large cubes
8 whole black peppercorns, lightly crushed
Pinch of kosher salt
2 ounces apple cider vinegar
2½ ounces sorghum molasses

Juice the butternut squash, then fine-strain into an airtight container and discard the solids. Let the juice sit in the fridge overnight, so that the starch settles to the bottom of the container. The next day, pour the juice into a fresh container, leaving behind the starch. You should have just over 1½ cups of squash juice.

In a small saucepan combine the juice and the black peppercorns. Simmer over low heat, then cook until the juice has reduced by half, 10 to 15 minutes. Remove from the heat and stir in the salt, vinegar, molasses, and 1½ ounces water. Let cool, then strain through a cheesecloth-lined strainer and discard the solids.

Store the shrub in an airtight container in the refrigerator for up to 1 month.

Note Removing or at least reducing the starch is VERY important; if you don't, the juice becomes yogurt-like in consistency as soon as you add even the slightest amount of heat. If you can't find sorghum molasses, maple syrup is a fine alternative.

Once More, with Feeling: On Carbonation

I know I wrote about this in the Tools section (see "Carbonator," page 20), but it's worth reiterating: Carbonate your drinks before sweetening them, especially if you're using a SodaStream.

If you try to carbonate sugary liquid, you'll end up producing foam. That foam will clog the machine and likely ultimately break it. Or you!

I'm only half kidding; this really can get dangerous. (Google "SodaStream explosion.") The method isn't ideal—by stirring in syrup post-carbonation, you'll knock out some effervescence—but safety is key.

If you're using an iSi soda siphon, though, there's a way around this. Head to bartender Jeffrey Morgenthaler's website jeffreymorgenthaler.com and search "How to Use an iSi Soda Siphon to Carbonate House-made Sodas." He'll show you the trick for safely and successfully carbonating sugary liquids.

If and only if you're using an iSi, and when and only when you've watched Jeffrey's video, you can try carbonating a drink into which the syrup has already been incorporated. Here's how the Cham-pine (facing page) method would change, accordingly: Mix the tea, acids, sugar, and honey while the tea is hot, then chill the Cham-pine, and, finally, carbonate it.

Good luck. And stay careful out there!

Cham-pine

ATERA — NEW YORK, NEW YORK

This was, four years ago, the first sophisticated nonalcoholic drink that stayed on my mind for weeks (months? years, apparently). It's effervescent, brightly acidic, and pine-y (yes, pine-y), and is delicious with caviar. The recipe may seem intimidating, but really, the hard part is gathering the ingredients. After that, it's just steeping and stirring. Atera's beverage director, Evan Manka, tells me he gets regular shipments of white pine from a special source, but if you live in a more rural area, you can just walk outside; the stuff grows everywhere. Some conifers, such as those in the Yew family, aren't safe to consume, so consult a foraging book before you go gathering. Buy the acids at modernistpantry.com.

COMMITMENT LEVEL ●●●●
SERVES 8

4	cups tightly packed fresh white pine needles
¼	cup sugar
¼	cup honey
¾	teaspoon tartaric acid
¾	teaspoon lactic acid
¼	teaspoon malic acid

Rinse the pine needles in cold water.

In a large stockpot, combine the pine needles and 6¼ cups water. Over the lowest heat your stovetop will allow, gently cook the mixture for 2½ hours. (The liquid won't even show signs of simmering; you're just looking to infuse the flavor.) Strain and discard the solids. Then strain the liquid a second time, using a tea strainer, to remove any bits of sediment.

While it's still hot, measure out ¼ cup of the pine tea and, in a separate bowl, mix it with the sugar and honey. (They should dissolve in the liquid at this temperature if you stir vigorously, but, if not, you can gently reheat the mixture in a saucepan.) Set aside the syrup and let it cool. Meanwhile, again while the remainder of the pine tea is warm, stir in the acids. Let the tea cool to room temperature, then chill thoroughly in the refrigerator.

Carbonate the pine infusion, then gently stir in the syrup. (If using an iSi, see the facing page.) Divide among 8 flutes.

Cucumber Doogh

HILLARY NEUMAN-RATIU — SARMA, SOMERVILLE, MASSACHUSETTS

When I was in Nashville, I stayed with the food writer Louisa Shafia. "DOOGH!" she exclaimed, as I walked in the door. Louisa is Persian, and she wanted to introduce me to the fizzy, salty, yogurt-y Middle Eastern drink. When I brought it up to my friend Andy Baraghani, who is also Persian, he said, "On hot summer days. With kebabs and grilled meats. The best." That was it; I had to find a recipe for doogh. This one is not traditional—it's flavored with cucumber instead of mint, it contains lime juice, and the salt is incorporated into the yogurt instead of sprinkled right into the glass— but I like it. And so did Andy when I made it for him. (Phew!)

COMMITMENT LEVEL ●○○○
SERVES 1

- 4 ounces soda water
- 2 ounces Cucumber-Rose Yogurt (recipe follows)
- ½ ounce freshly squeezed lime juice
- Dried rose petals, for garnish (optional)

Pour the soda water into a collins glass. Add the yogurt and lime juice and give it a quick stir, then fill with crushed ice. Top with more soda water, if you wish. Garnish with dried rose petals, if using.

Cucumber-Rose Yogurt

MAKES 1¼ CUPS, ENOUGH FOR 5 DRINKS

- 1 cup plain, full-fat Greek yogurt
- ½ cup chopped English or Persian cucumber
- 1 teaspoon kosher salt
- ½ teaspoon rose water (optional)

Combine the yogurt, cucumber, salt, rose water (if using), and 1¾ ounces water in a blender. Blend until smooth, then fine-strain and discard the solids. Store the yogurt in an airtight container in the refrigerator for up to 1 week.

Batch for 4 Combine 2 cups soda water, 1 cup yogurt, and ¼ cup freshly squeezed lime juice in a pitcher and gently stir. Divide among 4 collins glasses, then fill each with crushed ice. Garnish each with dried rose petals, if using.

Note Feel free to bump up the lime juice if you like things extra tart. (I do.)

Change of Address

ERIC NELSON — EEM, PORTLAND, OREGON

Eric Nelson doesn't take cocktails—or life, really—too seriously. Seriously! His drinks are well crafted, but they also have a sense of humor, and I love the way he doctors everyday Coca-Cola with savory soy sauce in this recipe. The drink is a killer pairing for a burger.

COMMITMENT LEVEL ●○○○
SERVES 1

¾ ounce freshly squeezed lemon juice
¾ ounce maple syrup
1 teaspoon soy sauce
3 ounces Coca-Cola
Freshly grated cinnamon, for garnish

Combine the lemon juice, maple syrup, and soy sauce in a cocktail shaker. Fill with ice, seal the shaker, and shake just to combine, about 3 seconds. Add the Coca-Cola, then double-strain into a collins glass filled with crushed ice. To serve, grate cinnamon over the top.

Bitters and Soda Water

Some people's go-to order is a gin and tonic. For *New York Times* food correspondent Kim Severson, it's soda with bitters and lemon.

That's my drink! The bitters stimulate the appetite; the drink contains the right amount of bitters when it turns pale pink. Sometimes the house-made versions can be too heavy on the alcohol, though. I think of bitters like charcuterie: For a while, every chef thought they could make it, and there was a lot of terrible charcuterie out there. You can't just hang a ham in your walk-in and it's going to turn out well! In the same way, now that everyone and their mother and father are making bitters, the results vary. I usually go for the tried-and-true Angostura brand.

Then there's the effervescence of the soda water: The bubbles almost clean your tongue. And, finally, lemon's acidity is sharp—lime's tropical notes are too much, in my opinion—so it's a good supporting character.

I like it in a big, sturdy rocks glass. It feels more cocktail-y, plus, people are less apt to put a straw in a rocks glass. (Politics aside, I just don't like drinking out of a straw.) At home, when I take a minute to prepare it at the end of the day, it's a nice transition moment for me. It says, 'Now is the time to settle down, have a little treat, and move into the next occasion.'

How to Make Bitters and Soda

Fill a glass with ice (or don't; up to you). Add chilled soda water, then add a couple dashes of bitters, whatever kind you like. Squeeze a lemon or lime wedge over it and drop it in the glass (or don't; up to you). That's it!

Or You Could Buy It

In the past couple of years, four canned bitters and soda products have come onto the scene: Angostura's Lemon, Lime, and Bitters; Dram's "herbal sparkling waters," which co-owner Shae Whitney flavors with her cardamom and black tea, lavender and lemon balm, or citrus bitters; Hella Cocktail Co.'s Bitters & Soda, which comes in two flavors, Aromatic Dry and Aromatic Spritz, both made with gentian root tinctures; and the Bitter Housewife's Bitters & Soda, flavored with dried cherries, sarsaparilla, and allspice, among other spices and barks. Note that some of them taste sweeter than the homemade version: Angostura's, for example, is akin to 7UP; and Dram's doesn't have any sugar, but the glycerin in the bitters registers as slightly sweet on the palate.

Up-Beet

BRANDYN TEPPER — ANGLER, SAN FRANCISCO, CALIFORNIA

Full body and robust tannins are what you get with this drink, which Angler's former beverage director, Brandyn Tepper, pairs with truffle-topped pasta or, in the summer, hanger steak with salsa verde. Like with wine, temperature is important here. I note to remove the drink from the refrigerator thirty-five minutes before serving, but on a hot day, it may warm more quickly. (If you want to get nerdy and take its temperature, it should be 55°F.)

COMMITMENT LEVEL ●●○○
SERVES 4

1	teaspoon loose-leaf oolong tea
½	cup just-boiled water
½	cup fresh beet juice
1½	cups pomegranate juice, preferably POM

In a heatproof bowl, combine the tea and the water and let it sit for 6 minutes. You may want to taste at the 3-minute mark to determine what level of bitterness you prefer, keeping in mind that it will ultimately be mixed with some pretty earthy, weighty ingredients. (I like it strong.) Strain the tea and let it cool completely.

In a large container, combine the tea, beet juice, and pomegranate juice and stir to combine. Cover and refrigerate until chilled, about 4 hours or up to 2 days.

Remove the drink from the refrigerator at least 35 minutes before serving and let it stand at room temperature. To serve, divide among 4 red wine glasses.

Note If you're making your own fresh beet juice, be sure to trim, wash, and cut the beets into chunks before running them through the juicer, then fine-strain the liquid. (Three-quarters of a pound of loose red beets should get you 4 to 5 ounces of liquid.) Otherwise, R. W. Knudsen makes good, organic beet juice.

Saffron Sharbat

KY BELK — EL FIVE, DENVER, COLORADO

Sharbat, a sweet drink made from fruit or flower petals, can be found in various forms from northern Africa through the Middle East, Central Asia, and India. At El Five, which serves Spanish/Turkish/Moroccan-ish/Israeli-ish tapas, bar director Ky Belk pairs this saffron version with classic paella, which—and I don't use this word lightly—is PERFECT. The verjus brings a soft acidity that tempers the sweetness, and soda water opens it all up without diluting the floral notes.

COMMITMENT LEVEL ●●○○
SERVES 1

2	ounces white verjus
½	ounce Saffron Sharbat Syrup (recipe follows)
4	ounces soda water
1	lemon twist, for garnish

In a tumbler filled with ice, combine the verjus and syrup. Top with the soda water and gently stir. Garnish with the lemon twist.

Saffron Sharbat Syrup

MAKES ABOUT 1 CUP, ENOUGH FOR 16 DRINKS

¼	teaspoon saffron threads
2	teaspoons just-boiled water
⅔	cup sugar
1	tablespoon plus 1 teaspoon orange flower water

Put the saffron in a small heatproof bowl, then pour the water over top. Let it steep for 15 minutes.

Combine the sugar and ½ cup water in a small saucepan, then add the saffron mixture and orange flower water. Simmer over low heat, stirring to dissolve the sugar, for 5 minutes. Remove from the heat, fine-strain and discard the solids, and let cool to room temperature. Store the syrup in an airtight container in the refrigerator for up to 1 week.

Batch for 6 Combine 1½ cups white verjus and 3 ounces syrup in a pitcher halfway filled with ice and stir well to combine. Add 3 cups soda water and gently stir again. To serve, pour into 6 tumblers and garnish each with a lemon twist.

Vinegar

Michael Harlan Turkell wrote the book on vinegar. (Seriously! It's called *Acid Trip: Travels in the World of Vinegar*.) Here, he shares why it's worth drinking.

Citrus degrades so quickly over time, but vinegar is this contiguous substance: from drink to drink and mixer to mixer, there's consistency. That helps my OCD.

I'm not an acid elitist, though. Lemons are what works in a whiskey sour. Every acid has its place.

Vinegar is a great flavor extractor and enhancer, and I like one with a bit of residual sugar to it. You'll get that in some rice vinegars and fruit vinegars, and sometimes in white wine vinegars. One producer, Katz, in Sonoma, makes such a nice late-harvest red wine vinegar, I just sip it straight. Or you could put a few dashes of any of these vinegars into seltzer, like you would with bitters. CO_2, the gas that makes seltzer effervescent, has some acid in it, too, so it's this great double-punch: sharpness from CO_2, and brightness from the vinegar.

Overall, vinegar is a good palate cleanser: You can start off a meal with it or drink it mid-course, as a refresher—and I've even used it as a digestive. That was really balsamico's first purpose!

Oregon Berry Drinking Vinegar

Chef Andy Ricker's drinking vinegars are so popular, he bottled them. You can buy any one of a range of Som flavors at somcordial.com, or try this recipe, which Ricker slipped me when I toured his factory in Portland. If you can't find coconut vinegar, any white, cane-based vinegar with a clean acidity will work; just avoid white balsamic, apple cider vinegar, or anything that has a strong flavor.

●○○○ MAKES 2 CUPS

½   cup blueberries
½   cup blackberries
1   cup strawberries, tops
     removed
1½   cups coconut vinegar
½   teaspoon sea salt
1   cup sugar
Soda water

In a nonreactive container such as a quart-size glass Ball jar, combine the blueberries, blackberries, and strawberries. Smash the berries with the back of a wooden spoon, then add the vinegar and stir. Cover and let the mixture sit at room temperature for 48 hours.

Fine-strain the liquid into a saucepan and discard the solids. Warm the liquid over medium heat, bringing it just to a simmer. Add the salt and sugar, stirring to combine, then remove the pan from the heat and let the vinegar cool to room temperature. The drinking vinegar can be stored in the refrigerator for up to 1 year.

To drink, mix ½ ounce berry vinegar with 4 ounces soda water. Serve with or without ice.

Earth & Leaf

JULIA MOMOSE — KUMIKO, CHICAGO, ILLINOIS

"Have you talked to Julia Momose?" Almost every bartender I spoke with for this book pointed me her way, and I quickly learned that she's one of the best when it comes to nonalcoholic cocktails, which she calls "Spiritfrees" (see page 9). The Spiritfrees at her restaurant, Kumiko, are meant to be paired with food; this one, she says, works with robust dishes like steak or roasted beets, and the sesame oil lends itself to Chinese and Japanese dishes such as *mapo tofu* or *sukiyaki*.

COMMITMENT LEVEL ●●○○
SERVES 1

1   ounce Seedlip Garden 108
      (see page 29)
1   ounce chilled hōjicha tea
¾   ounce red verjus
¼   ounce Simple Syrup
      (page 37)
1   lemon twist for garnish
Toasted sesame oil

Combine the Seedlip, tea, verjus, and simple syrup in a mixing glass. Fill with ice and stir for 15 seconds, until well chilled. Strain into a chilled coupe. Squeeze the lemon twist over the drink to express its oil, then discard. Finish with a drop of sesame oil.

Batch for 6 In a pitcher, combine ¾ cup Seedlip Garden 108, ¾ cup *hōjicha*, ½ cup plus 1 tablespoon red verjus, 3 tablespoons simple syrup, and ¼ cup filtered water. Stir to combine, then refrigerate until thoroughly chilled. (The mixture will stay good stored in an airtight container in the refrigerator for up to 3 days.) Divide among 6 chilled coupes, squeeze a lemon twist over each and discard, and finish each with a drop of sesame oil.

Note You can find *hōjicha*, Japanese roasted green tea, at Harney & Sons (harney .com) or kettl.co. You'll also use it to make the Fuyu (page 158). Seedlip is available at some specialty stores and at seedlipdrinks.com/us.

El Curandero

LANE HARLAN — CLAVEL, BALTIMORE, MARYLAND

Lane Harlan is not so quietly reshaping Baltimore's drinking scene with her speakeasy-style bar, W.C. Harlan (see the recipe for Lorca on page 81), and, down the street, her more minimalist mezcaleria and Sinaloan restaurant, Clavel. (As I had so very badly hoped, John Waters is a regular.) Drink this earthy, spicy shrub with—duh!—tacos.

COMMITMENT LEVEL ●●●○
SERVES 1

Tajín Clásico or other chile-lime seasoning powder
1 lime wedge
1 ounce freshly squeezed lime juice
½ ounce Tres Chiles Shrub (recipe follows)
5 ounces soda water, preferably Topo Chico
1 lime twist for garnish

Pour the Tajín into a small, shallow bowl. Rub the lime wedge around the rim of a collins glass, then dip the glass into the Tajín. Fill the spice-rimmed glass with ice, then add the lime juice and shrub. Top with soda water and garnish with a lime twist.

Tres Chiles Shrub
MAKES 1 QUART, ENOUGH FOR 64 DRINKS

2 large ancho chiles
2 large guajillo chiles
2 large pasilla chiles
½ small serrano pepper
¼ habanero pepper
1 cinnamon stick
¼ cup cacao nibs
1 quart unfiltered, unpasteurized apple cider vinegar, such as Bragg's
2½ cups packed light brown sugar

In a saucepan, combine the ancho, guajillo, and pasilla chiles with the serrano and habanero peppers, cinnamon, and cacao. Cover with the vinegar and bring to a boil over medium-high heat. Decrease the heat to a bare simmer and cook, stirring occasionally, until the chiles have swelled, about 30 minutes. Remove from the heat, immediately add the sugar, and stir to combine.

Let the mixture cool completely, then fine-strain into a bowl or other container and discard the solids. Store the shrub in an airtight container in the refrigerator for up to 1 month.

Batch for 6 You've got enough of the shrub to serve six people and then some! Instead of rimming the glasses with Tajín, it might be easier to garnish with it. So, fill 6 collins glasses with ice, then add 1 ounce lime juice and ½ ounce shrub to each, top each with soda water, and stir gently to mix. Sprinkle some Tajín on top of each drink. There's less fuss and it still hits the lips with some heat. Garnish each with a lime twist.

Pea Flower Lemonade

NICK WISEMAN — LITTLE SESAME, WASHINGTON, D.C.

There is performance art involved, here! Dried butterfly pea flowers naturally dye water blue, but when you add citric acid, the liquid turns *purple*. That's why the lemon juice comes at the end of the process. If you're serving a crowd, you could even bring out shot glasses of lemon juice (or a bunch of lemon halves in a bowl) and let your guests add their own. It really is fun to watch the drink change color. This pairs well with hummus, harissa-rubbed meats—anything Middle Eastern, really.

COMMITMENT LEVEL ●○○○
SERVES 6

2¼   teaspoons coriander seeds
2½   tablespoons dried butterfly pea flowers
½   cup turbinado sugar
6   cups just-boiled water
3   tablespoons freshly squeezed lemon juice

Toast the coriander seeds in a small sauté pan over medium-low heat, stirring frequently to prevent burning, about 3 minutes. Transfer the seeds to a plate and let cool completely. Crack in a mortar and pestle (or nestle the seeds in a kitchen towel and crush them with the bottom of a heavy pan).

Combine the dried flowers, sugar, and coriander seeds in a large heatproof bowl or pitcher. Pour the water over the ingredients and stir, then allow them to steep for 30 minutes. Fine-strain, discard the solids, and let the tea cool to room temperature, then cover and refrigerate until chilled, about 2 hours. Store in an airtight container in the refrigerator for up to 1 week.

To serve, divide the tea among 6 collins glasses filled with ice. Add 1½ teaspoons of the lemon juice to each glass. (You could add all 3 tablespoons of lemon juice to the tea base at once, for ease, but, like I said, it's fun to let your guests watch the transformation!)

Note The chefs at Little Sesame order Doi Thai–brand butterfly pea flowers through Amazon. Wherever you buy them, they're likely coming from Thailand, where they're grown, so it might take them some time to arrive at your doorstep. Plan accordingly!

Sparkling Tarragon Cider

PIPER KRISTENSEN — OXALIS, BROOKLYN, NEW YORK

Oxalis goes through a *lot* of chervil, and the stems are what beverage director Piper Kristensen uses to infuse classic Martinelli's apple juice with a delicate herbal flavor. I prefer the punchiness of tarragon, which is more readily available, and I use the stems and the leaves so that the anise flavor really comes through. The proverbial cherry on top—the final note to this drink that makes it sing—is the Champagne Acid. It makes the sides of your tongue water in the best way. Piper pairs this drink with a white asparagus appetizer, but steamed artichokes would be good, too.

COMMITMENT LEVEL ●●○○
SERVES 8

25 sprigs of tarragon
1   cup just-boiled water
3   cups apple juice, such as Martinelli's
3   ounces Champagne Acid (recipe follows)

Put the tarragon into a medium heatproof bowl and pour the water over it, pressing the herbs to submerge them. Let it sit until the tea cools to room temperature, about 30 minutes, then strain. Discard the solids.

Combine the tarragon tea with the apple juice and acid. Refrigerate to chill thoroughly. (The mixture will keep, un-carbonated, in an airtight container in the refrigerator for up to 1 week.) Carbonate the cider and serve in white wine glasses.

Champagne Acid

¼   teaspoon lactic acid
¼   teaspoon tartaric acid

In a small bowl, whisk 3 ounces water with the acids until they're dissolved.

Note You'll notice that the Cham-pine, from Atera restaurant (page 127), contains malic, lactic, and tartaric acids, and this recipe calls for just the latter two. Sometimes champagne goes through malolactic fermentation, during which tart malic acid converts into softer lactic acid, and sometimes it doesn't. The bartenders at Atera like how round the flavors are when all three acids are present; Piper prefers the leanness of just the two. (Plus, apple juice naturally contains malic acid.)

Nighttime

Whether they stand in for dessert or help cap a long night, these drinks are meant to be enjoyed when it's dark out and the stars are twinkling. Another hour, and you'll be fast asleep— or on a dance floor somewhere.

Sea Salt Shakerato

SAHRA NGUYEN — NGUYEN COFFEE SUPPLY, BROOKLYN, NEW YORK

Sahra Nguyen is on a mission to turn people on to the dark, nutty flavor profile of robusta coffee, of which her parents' native Vietnam is the largest producer. (In fact, you can buy some beans that she roasts herself, at nguyencoffeesupply.com.) Arabica beans would have a hard time standing up to the milks in this drink, which is a play on an Italian espresso shakerato. The sea salt is a nod to Sahra's mother, who was born in a Vietnamese fishing village. I think the drink is a great post-dinner dessert coffee, but I've also been known to take it with my breakfast (!).

COMMITMENT LEVEL ●●OO
SERVES 1

2½   ounces Phin Coffee
      (recipe follows)
½   ounce whole milk
¾   ounce sweetened
      condensed milk
Small pinch of coarse sea salt

Combine the coffee, whole milk, sweetened condensed milk, and salt in a cocktail shaker. Fill with ice, seal the shaker, and shake for 10 to 15 seconds, until well chilled. Place a single large ice cube in a rocks glass and double-strain the shakerato into the glass.

Phin Coffee

MAKES 2½ OUNCES, ENOUGH FOR 1 DRINK

2   tablespoons medium-fine
     ground coffee
3   ounces hot water

Spoon the ground coffee into the phin's (see note below) main chamber and give it a little shake. (This will help the grounds settle evenly.)

Place the phin atop a small bowl or a mug, then screw in the press. (This will further level out the grounds and encourage even drainage.) Screw it until it's snug, then back it off one turn.

Add half of the water into the phin and wait 20 seconds. (This will moisten the coffee, or "bloom" the grounds.) Add the remaining water and place the lid on top. It should take 3 to 4 minutes to brew; if the water drains more quickly than that, your grind is too coarse. Conversely, if the water hasn't all passed through the filter after 4 minutes, then your grind is too fine.

Remove the phin from your mug and enjoy.

Note Using a phin may take a little practice, but once you get it, you *get it*. Sahra describes the method as the intersection between a French press and a pour-over. Buy a small one of these metal coffee filters, ubiquitous in Vietnam, for around five bucks online. It has three parts: the main piece, which includes the brewing chamber and a lip, to help it sit atop a mug (sometimes these come in two parts, the brewing chamber and a separate plate that it sits upon); a press; and the lid.

Digesteaf

SARA KAUFMAN — STEVEN SMITH TEAMAKER, PORTLAND, OREGON

In Portland, I fell in love with a tea. Steven Smith Teamaker's Astoria's Amaro is a bitter, sweet, floral, smooth herbal tea meant to mimic an Italian amaro. Turns out, it was a limited-edition product. But the people at Smith are extremely generous: They created a DIY version of the tea so that I (we!) could make it at home. The recipe requires sourcing various dried roots and such (try mountainroseherbs.com and remediesherbshop.com), but the end product is like nothing I've tasted in the nonalcoholic realm: With almost every sip, it morphs from bitter to sweet and then back again. I like sipping the Astoria's Amaro concentrate chilled, just on its own, but if you need something tamer, try it in the Digesteaf cocktail.

COMMITMENT LEVEL ●●●●
SERVES 4

1	cup tonic water
¾	cup Astoria's Amaro Concentrate (recipe follows)
1½	ounces Simple Syrup (page 37)
4	dashes of lavender bitters
2	lemon wedges

Divide the tonic water among 4 small whiskey glasses. Combine the concentrate, simple syrup, and bitters in a cocktail shaker. Squeeze the lemon wedges over the mixture and add them to the shaker. Fill with ice, seal the shaker, and shake for 10 to 15 seconds, until well chilled. Strain, dividing evenly among the 4 glasses.

Astoria's Amaro Concentrate

MAKES ¾ CUP, ENOUGH FOR
4 DRINKS

1	teaspoon chicory root
2	teaspoons ashwagandha root
2	tablespoons pink rose petals
2	teaspoons rooibos tea leaves
1	packed teaspoon dried artichoke leaves
1	teaspoon honeybush tea
½	teaspoon licorice root
1	packed tablespoon freshly grated orange zest
1	cup just-boiled water

In a medium heatproof bowl, combine the chicory root, ashwagandha root, rose petals, rooibos tea, artichoke leaves, honeybush tea, licorice root, and orange zest. Pour in the water and let steep, uncovered, for 5 minutes. Fine-strain, discard the solids, and let cool. Store in an airtight container in the refrigerator for up to 2 days.

Note For a sweeter tea concentrate, increase the amount of licorice root. For a more bitter amaro tea, increase the amount of artichoke leaves.

Cold-Fashioned

JONATHAN ECHEVERRY — PAPER PLANE COFFEE CO., MONTCLAIR, NEW JERSEY

It looks like an old-fashioned, it sips slow like an old-fashioned, but it's a *Cold*-Fashioned, made with cold-brew concentrate instead of rye or bourbon. Jonathan Echeverry's family has been growing coffee in Colombia for about 150 years, and his flagship Dogma blend (paperplanecoffee.com), which is 60 percent Brazilian beans, 20 percent Colombian, and 20 percent Ethiopian, is as complex as a spirit. "Whiskey is usually a blend, too," he says. "The chocolaty Brazilian gives it body, the citrusy Colombian brings out the orange, and the fruit-forward Ethiopian blends with the cherry." Make your own cold-brew concentrate using his beans, or buy it pre-made (I used Grady's brand). Jonathan recommends the Cold-Fashioned as a pick-me-up after dinner.

COMMITMENT LEVEL ●○○○
SERVES 1

½   ounce turbinado simple syrup (use the same method for Simple Syrup, page 37)
1   half-moon orange slice
1   maraschino cherry
3   dashes Angostura bitters
4   ounces cold-brew concentrate
1   orange twist, for garnish

Combine the syrup, orange slice, cherry, and bitters in a cocktail shaker and muddle. Add the cold brew, seal the shaker, and shake to combine, about 3 seconds. Strain into a rocks glass filled with one large ice cube. Garnish with the orange twist.

Batch for 6 Muddle 3 ounces syrup, 3 orange slices, 6 cherries, and 2¼ teaspoons bitters in a pitcher. Add 3 cups cold-brew concentrate and stir to combine. Strain among 6 rocks glasses, each one filled with one large ice cube. Garnish each with an orange twist.

Golden Hour

JON PALMER — BACHELOR FARMER, MINNEAPOLIS, MINNESOTA

Jon Palmer wanted to mimic a late-harvest wine with his Golden Hour, and I think he succeeded. To me, it tastes and feels like Sauternes, in terms of sweetness and viscosity, and the honey and simple syrups work in concert to achieve that. Speaking of sweet: It definitely is! This is meant to be like a dessert wine, so sip slowly.

COMMITMENT LEVEL ●●○○
SERVES 1

2	ounces white verjus
¾	ounce Rich Honey Syrup (page 37)
¼	ounce Simple Syrup (page 37)
½	teaspoon orange flower water

Combine the verjus, syrups, and orange flower water in a mixing glass. Fill with ice and stir for 15 seconds, until well chilled. Strain into a chilled coupe.

Batch for 6 Combine 1½ cups white verjus, ½ cup plus 1 tablespoon honey syrup, 3 tablespoons simple syrup, and 1 tablespoon orange flower water in a pitcher and stir. Chill in the refrigerator for at least 2 hours. To serve, divide among 6 chilled coupes.

Note Buy Fusion brand white verjus at chefshop.com.

Cherry & Smoke

EVAN ZIMMERMAN — WASHINGTON, D.C.

I first met Evan when I interviewed him about the drinks he concocted for a five-course dinner put on by an all-star lineup of sober chefs. He has since become a friend, doubling as a drinks tutor, and while he offered up a zillion ideas for this book, the simplicity and versatility of the Cherry & Smoke won me over. The campfire smokiness of the Lapsang Souchong, which he brews strong, so that the tannins intensify, is such a good counterpoint to the sweet, tart stone fruit. Speaking of the cherry juice: Use a clarified version, such as Lakewood brand. (I tested this recipe using Trader Joe's cherry juice, which is cloudier, and it didn't work as well.) You can serve this drink warm or chilled, and while Evan (and I!) prefer it as a nightcap, it would suit barbecue, too.

COMMITMENT LEVEL ●○○○
SERVES 1

½	teaspoon loose-leaf Lapsang Souchong tea
3	ounces just-boiled water
3	ounces tart cherry juice
1	lemon twist, for garnish

In a small heatproof bowl, combine the tea and the water, then cover and let sit for 5 minutes. Stir in the cherry juice, then immediately fine-strain into a snifter. Squeeze the lemon twist over the drink to express its oils, then discard. Serve warm.

Batch for 6 In a medium heatproof bowl, combine 1 tablespoon tea and 2¼ cups water, then cover and let sit for 5 minutes. Stir in 2¼ cups cherry juice and immediately fine-strain into 6 snifters (or, honestly, whatever glasses you have). Squeeze lemon twists over each drink (2 will do you), then discard. Serve warm.

Fuyu

OLIVIA NOREN AND JONATHAN MACAHON — YŪGEN, CHICAGO, ILLINOIS

I allowed only one egg cocktail into this book. There's no explanation other than that I'm just not a huge fan of eggs in drinks, but my research associate, Coral Lee, committed to testing this recipe five times to get it right (and to prove me wrong). Coral is more than ten years my junior, is an exponentially better cook, and will hopefully one day be my boss, so I'll let her explain what she loves about the Fuyu: "This is everything eggnog should be but isn't: toasty and insanely creamy with a kick from the fresh ginger juice. Yes, it requires effort, but taste it and then tell me if it was too much. You—*ahem, Julia*—won't." I submit! That said, I did test this drink without the egg, and it still works. Coral approves of the "optional" note.

COMMITMENT LEVEL ●●●○
SERVES 1

2 ounces Seedlip Spice 94 (see sidebar, page 29)
1 ounce Black Sesame Cream (recipe follows)
1½ ounces Hōjicha-Ginger Syrup (recipe follows)
1 large egg (optional)
Black sesame seeds, either whole or crushed between your fingers, for garnish

Combine the Seedlip, cream, syrup, and egg, if using, in a cocktail shaker. Seal and shake for 10 to 15 seconds. Open the shaker, add ice, seal again, and shake for 10 to 15 seconds, until well chilled. (If you're not using the egg, you can skip the first step, called a "dry shake," and simply shake with ice from the get-go.) Double-strain into a coupe and finish with the sesame seeds.

Black Sesame Cream

MAKES ¾ CUP, ENOUGH FOR 6 DRINKS

¼ cup black sesame seeds
1 cup heavy cream

In a small saucepan, combine the sesame seeds and cream and, over medium-low heat, bring just to a simmer. Remove from the heat and let cool to room temperature, then strain and discard the solids. Store the cream in an airtight container in the refrigerator for up to 3 days.

CONTINUED

Note Find *hōjicha*, a Japanese roasted green tea, at Harney & Sons (harney.com). If you enjoy it in this drink, try the Earth & Leaf (page 140).

Fuyu

CONTINUED

Hōjicha-Ginger Syrup
MAKES 1¹/₂ CUPS, ENOUGH FOR
8 DRINKS

1   cup dark muscovado
     sugar
⅓   cup loose-leaf hōjicha tea
½   cup fresh ginger juice

In a small saucepan, combine
1 cup water, the sugar, and the
tea. Bring to a simmer, stirring
to combine, then remove from
the heat and let sit for 30 minutes. Stir in the ginger juice and
then fine-strain, pressing on the
solids to extract as much liquid
as possible. Discard the solids.
Store the syrup in an airtight
container in the refrigerator for
up to 2 weeks.

Rose & Kumquat

HANSUK CHO — DIALOGUE, SANTA MONICA, CALIFORNIA

Hansuk Cho is like the nonalcoholic drinks whisperer of California. She's worked at fine-dining restaurants SingleThread in Sonoma (try the Pear Cider on page 106), Dialogue in Santa Monica, and she has plans to teach other bartenders some of her tricks. But we got to her first! Hansuk recommends pairing this drink with lychees, peaches, pumpkin, or squash, and while all of that makes perfect sense to me, I also like it on its own. The lean mouthfeel, the floral notes, the gravity that the tea brings—it's an elegant finish to a very long day.

COMMITMENT LEVEL ●○○○
SERVES 3

1   teaspoon loose-leaf black tea, such as Assam or English Breakfast
1   tablespoon finely chopped fresh lemongrass
1   cup just-boiled water
Dash of rose water
1   ounce Kumquat Syrup (recipe follows)

In a medium heatproof bowl, combine the tea, lemongrass, and the water and let sit for 2 minutes. Fine-strain and discard the solids, add the rose water, and let the liquid cool.

Combine the tea and syrup in a mixing glass. Fill with ice and stir for 15 seconds, until well chilled. Strain into 3 chilled coupes.

Kumquat Syrup

MAKES ¾ CUP, ENOUGH FOR
6 DRINKS

1   cup kumquats, halved crosswise
¼   cup honey
¾   cup sugar

Combine the kumquats, honey, and sugar in a bowl and mash the kumquats with the back of a wooden spoon. Cover and let sit at room temperature for 24 to 48 hours, stirring every so often, until the sugar has dissolved completely. Strain, discarding the fruit, and store the syrup in an airtight container in the fridge for up to 2 weeks.

Batch for 6 In a medium heatproof bowl, combine 2 teaspoons black tea, 2 tablespoons finely chopped fresh lemongrass, and 2 cups water and let sit for 2 minutes. Strain, discarding the solids; add 2 dashes of rose water; and let the liquid cool. Combine the tea and syrup in a pitcher. Fill with ice and stir for 15 seconds, until well chilled. Strain into 6 coupes.

Rhapsody in Blue

ROBERT MURPHY — EXISTING CONDITIONS, NEW YORK, NEW YORK

How cared-for would you feel if you went to a dinner party and, after dessert, your host poured a round of chilled juice that he or she had infused with spices in advance? What an extra little treat; what a gesture. Robert Murphy had vermouth in mind when he developed this recipe; the drink should be served in small glasses, just 2 ounces per person. I used the R.W. Knudsen brand of blueberry juice, which can be found at most grocery stores, but whatever you buy, make sure it's unsweetened and without preservatives. You want the body and acidity that only all-natural juice can bring.

COMMITMENT LEVEL ●ooo
SERVES 6

8   cardamom pods
3   star anise pods
2½   cups blueberry juice
2   strips of orange peel
      (no white pith), 2 to
      3 inches long

In a medium saucepan, combine the spices and toast them over medium-high heat, occasionally shaking the pan back and forth to prevent burning, until they're fragrant, 2 to 3 minutes. Transfer to a plate and let cool completely, 5 to 10 minutes, then transfer the toasted spices to a spice grinder and blend into a fine powder.

Using the same saucepan, combine the powdered spices with the blueberry juice and orange peels. Bring to a simmer over medium-high heat, then decrease to a gentle simmer and cook for 10 minutes. Fine-strain the liquid, discard the solids, and let it cool. Refrigerate to chill thoroughly, about 2 hours. To serve, divide among 6 cordial glasses.

The Rockefeller

JERMAINE WHITEHEAD — DEEP DIVE, SEATTLE, WASHINGTON

Here's an example of when replicating a classic cocktail works. As I mentioned in the introduction, I resisted that approach at first, but Jermaine (who has moved on to Il Nido in Seattle) captures what is so beloved about the Manhattan—the weight on the palate, the warming aromatics, the throat tickle (it comes from Urfa biber, a Turkish chile pepper, in this case)—and turns it into an after-dinner cocktail. I wouldn't recommend drinking the extra-bitter citrus water on its own, but balanced by the sweetness of the vermouth, this is a solid stirred drink, a rarity in the nonalcoholic realm. Speaking of the vermouth, if you make it in advance and chill it, bring it up to room-ish temperature before preparing the drink. Otherwise, it's too thick. The citrus water intensifies as it sits in the fridge, so you may want to recalibrate the ratios as you near the end of your bottle; by week three, I preferred a one-to-one mix.

COMMITMENT LEVEL ●●●●
SERVES 1

¾ ounce Vermouth (recipe follows)
3 ounces Citrus Water (recipe follows)
1 Luxardo cherry, for garnish

Combine the vermouth and citrus water in a mixing glass. Fill with ice and stir for 15 seconds, until well chilled. Strain into a chilled Nick & Nora glass and garnish with a Luxardo cherry.

Vermouth

MAKES ABOUT 1 CUP, ENOUGH FOR 8 DRINKS

2¼ teaspoons whole dried juniper berries
¾ teaspoon whole cloves
¾ teaspoon whole fennel seeds
¾ teaspoon whole black peppercorns
1½ teaspoons dried and crushed Urfa biber
¼ teaspoon vanilla extract
¼ teaspoon citric acid
2 cinnamon sticks
1½ cups red verjus
¾ cup sugar

In a nonreactive 4-quart saucepan, combine the juniper berries, cloves, fennel seeds, peppercorns, Urfa biber, vanilla, citric acid, cinnamon, verjus, and sugar.
CONTINUED

The Rockefeller

CONTINUED

Over medium-high heat, bring just to a boil, then decrease to a bare simmer and cook for 30 minutes. Remove from the heat, fine-strain and discard the solids, and cool. Store the vermouth in an airtight container in the refrigerator for up to 1 month.

Citrus Water

MAKES 3 CUPS, ENOUGH FOR 10 DRINKS

8	oranges
8	lemons
4	grapefruits
1	whole nutmeg
1	teaspoon whole cloves
1	cinnamon stick
1	tablespoon vanilla extract

Remove the peels from the oranges, lemons, and grapefruits in long strips, avoiding the white pith. Reserve the meat for another use.

In a 4-quart saucepan, combine the citrus peels with the nutmeg, cloves, cinnamon, vanilla, and 4 cups water. Bring just to a simmer over medium heat; decrease the heat to the lowest setting and cook at a bare simmer (bubbles should be just barely breaking the surface) until reduced to 3 cups, about 45 minutes. Fine-strain the liquid into a bowl, discard the solids, and let cool. Store the citrus water in an airtight container in the refrigerator for up to 1 month.

Batch for 6 Combine ½ cup plus 1 tablespoon vermouth and 2¼ cups citrus water in a pitcher filled with ice, and stir until thoroughly chilled, about 15 seconds. Strain, dividing among 6 Nick & Nora glasses (or whatever else you want to use). Garnish each with a Luxardo cherry.

Note Jermaine likes using citric acid in the vermouth for its direct, clean tartness and consistency. Buy it at modernistpantry.com.

The Umstead

ZACK THOMAS — CRAWFORD AND SON, RALEIGH, NORTH CAROLINA

Around the end of July, both mushrooms and blackberries can be found growing in Raleigh's William B. Umstead State Park. That's why, even though those two ingredients may sound strange paired together, Zack Thomas decided to try. "If it grows together, it goes together," he says. Turns out, it does: the blackberries are sweet and tart, and the mushrooms have an earthy, nutty quality that balances out the drink. Because it's slightly creamy from the yogurt, Zack likes the Umstead—yes, named for the park—after dinner, but it could go with brunch, too.

COMMITMENT LEVEL ●●○○
SERVES 1

1½ ounces Blackberry Syrup (recipe follows)
1½ ounces Maitake Mushroom Tea (recipe follows)
1 teaspoon Greek yogurt
Small pinch of sea salt
3–4 ounces soda water

Combine the syrup, tea, yogurt, and salt in a cocktail shaker. Fill with ice, seal the shaker, and shake for 10 to 15 seconds, until well chilled. Double-strain into a collins glass and top with soda water.

Blackberry Syrup
MAKES 1¾ CUPS, ENOUGH FOR 9 DRINKS

1 cup blackberries
1 cup sugar

In a small saucepan over medium heat, combine the blackberries, sugar, and 1 cup water. Bring to a simmer, stirring to dissolve the sugar and using the back of a wooden spoon to break up the berries.

Remove from the heat and let cool, then fine-strain and discard the solids. Store the syrup in an airtight container in the refrigerator for up to 1 week.

Maitake Mushroom Tea
MAKES ⅔ CUP, ENOUGH FOR 3 DRINKS

1 cup dehydrated maitake mushrooms
1 cup just-boiled water

In a medium, heatproof bowl, add the mushrooms and pour the water over them; press the mushrooms to submerge. Let steep for 15 minutes, then strain and discard the solids. Store the tea in an airtight container in the refrigerator for 2 to 3 days.

Bars to Try

The bars and restaurants that contributed recipes to this book don't necessarily make up a list of the best nonalcoholic cocktail programs in the country. They're all doing an excellent job, of course, but there are many more.

Here is a fuller list of places to drink and drink well, organized by state. (The bars and restaurants already referenced in this book have asterisks next to them.)

Please do a quick Google search before you go; some of these are bars, some are cafés, some are open just for lunch, some are tasting menu–only restaurants, and I want you to have the experience you're looking for (and to show up when the place is open!).

Cheers!

CALIFORNIA

Elk
Harbor House
    Inn*

Healdsburg
SingleThread*

Los Angeles
Angler
Bavel
Botanica
Destroyer
Go Get Em Tiger*
Omni
Providence
Redbird*
Republique
Sqirl
Trois Mec

San Francisco
Angler*
Horsefeather
Mourad
School Night*
Quince*
Trick Dog
True Laurel

Santa Monica
Dialogue*

COLORADO

Aurora
Annette

Boulder
Corrida*

Denver
Death & Co*
El Five*
Hudson Hill*
Lady Jane*

GEORGIA

Atlanta
Mission and
    Market*
Ticonderoga
    Club

Athens
The Expat

HAWAII

Maui
Lineage

ILLINOIS

Chicago
Acadia*
The Aviary
Elizabeth
Elske
Kumiko*
Lost Lake*
Spinning J
Yūgen*

INDIANA

Bloomington
C3*

Indianapolis
Milktooth

LOUISIANA

New Orleans
Compère Lapin
Jewel of the
    South
Saba

MAINE

Portland
Baharat
Vena's Fizz House

MARYLAND

Baltimore
Clavel*
W.C. Harlan*
Woodberry
    Kitchen

MASSACHUSETTS

Boston
Mei Mei

Cambridge
Alden & Harlow

Somerville
Sarma*

MICHIGAN

Detroit
Castalia at
    Sfumato*
Selden Standard
Willis Show Bar

MINNESOTA

Minneapolis
The Bachelor
    Farmer*
Colita
Hai Hai
Martina
Marvel Bar

MISSOURI

St. Louis
Vicia*

Kansas City
Corvino Supper
    Club*

NEVADA

Las Vegas
Starboard Tack
Velveteen Rabbit

NEW JERSEY

Montclair
Paper Plane
    Coffee Co.*

NEW YORK

New York City
abcV
Agern
Atera*
Atla
Blue Hill
The Bonnie*
Crown Shy
Dante*
Eleven Madison
    Park
Existing
    Conditions*
Getaway
Listen Bar*
Nitecap
Oxalis*
Pouring Ribbons
Reception Bar*
Wayla

Pocantico Hills
Blue Hill at Stone
    Barns

**NORTH
CAROLINA**

Asheville
Posana
Rhubarb

Durham
Kingfisher*

Raleigh
Crawford and
    Son*
Garland

OKLAHOMA

Oklahoma City
Nonesuch

OREGON

Portland
Beast
Clyde Common*
Departure*
Eem*
Guero*
Le Pigeon
Pok Pok
Quaintrelle
Steven Smith
    Teamaker*

PENNSYLVANIA

Philadelphia
Friday Saturday
    Sunday
ITV
Spice Finch
Suraya
Royal Boucherie
Vedge*
Zahav

**SOUTH
CAROLINA**

Charleston
Basic Kitchen
McCrady's
The Ordinary

TENNESSEE

Nashville
The Catbird Seat
High Garden Tea
Husk

Walland
Blackberry
    Mountain

TEXAS

Austin
Emmer and Rye
Garage Cocktail
    Bar

Houston
Coltivare*
Yauatcha

VIRGINIA

Richmond
Pomona*

WASHINGTON

Seattle
Deep Dive*
London Plane
Mr. West Cafe Bar

**WASHINGTON,
D.C.**

Columbia Room
The Dabney*
Fiola
The Green Zone
Hank's*
Little Sesame*
Pineapple and
    Pearls
Silver Lyan

Acknowledgments

To my friends: Thank you for seeing me, and for granting me permission to see you. What a privilege it is.

Mom and Dad! You've done a good job.

Thank you, Coral Lee, for letting me lean on you more than I should have. I can't wait to follow your career. Thank you, Mindy Fox, for helping me wrestle with these recipes.

Thank you, Ten Speed Press, for giving us this opportunity. Thanks especially to my editor, Kelly Snowden, who believed in this book and in me, even when I tried to convince her that I didn't know what I was doing. (I did! I do.) My agent, Stacey Glick, also somehow stuck around. Bless you, Stacey!

Thank you, Emma Campion, Chaz Capobianco, Elle Jaime, Alex Lau, Mike Ley, Sue Li, and Catherine Yoo, for making this book look so good. (It really does.)

Thanks to the drinks experts who shared their knowledge with me, among them Derek Brown, Ryan Chetiyawardana, John deBary, Camper English, Josh Harris, Maggie Hoffman, Emma Janzen, Drew Lazor, Jim Meehan, Brad Thomas Parsons, Matt Poli, Emily Timberlake, Samantha Weiss-Hills, and Evan Zimmerman. (Maggie deserves extra props for answering many anxious phone calls while she was moving her family across the country.) Thanks also to Fabian von Hauske for texting with me about agar from London when you were cooking for a pop-up and had limited time even to sleep. Daniela Galarza: the kumquat assist! A key move. Thank you, Blake MacKay, for helping me think through important pieces of this work. Megan Krigbaum: YOU! <3 Andy Baraghani, thanks for coming over and tasting. I love you.

Thank you to the many many many fellow food and drinks writers who talked to me about this book in some way, shape, or form. The list is too long to fit here, but you'll be hearing from me.

Thanks to all of you who tagged me on Instagram posts or DM'd me drink menus or otherwise alerted me to happenings in this space. Your enthusiasm (and your intel!) kept me going.

Thank you to the friends who put me up during my long, strange trip: Kimberly Chou Tsun An, Sara Dickerman, Lizz Gregory, Martha Holmberg, Daniel Khasidy, Mary Elizabeth King, Scott Peacock, Louisa Shafia, Alex Shapiro, Michaele Smith (and Mackenzie Smith Kelley!), Celia Soehner, and Hannah Sullivan.

Thanks to all the bartenders who contributed to this book— and to the many more who submitted recipes or met me for a drink.

Thank you to Mickey Bakst, Sean Brock, Katie Button, Scott Crawford, Gregory Gourdet, Matthew Jennings, Kat Kinsman, Steve Palmer, Gabriel Rucker, Michael Solomonov, Philip Speer, and others for supporting the well-being of people working in the hospitality industry.

Thank you to hospitality workers for taking care of us.

Index

All rights reserved.
Published in the United States
by Ten Speed Press, an imprint
of Random House, a division of
Penguin Random House LLC,
New York.
www.tenspeed.com

Ten Speed Press and the Ten
Speed Press colophon are
registered trademarks of Penguin
Random House LLC.

Library of Congress
Cataloging-in-Publication Data
is on file with the publisher.

Hardcover ISBN: 978-1-9848-5634-0
eBook ISBN: 978-1-9848-5635-7

Printed in China

Design by Mike Ley
Food styling by Sue Li
Prop styling by Elle Jaime

10 9 8 7 6 5

First Edition

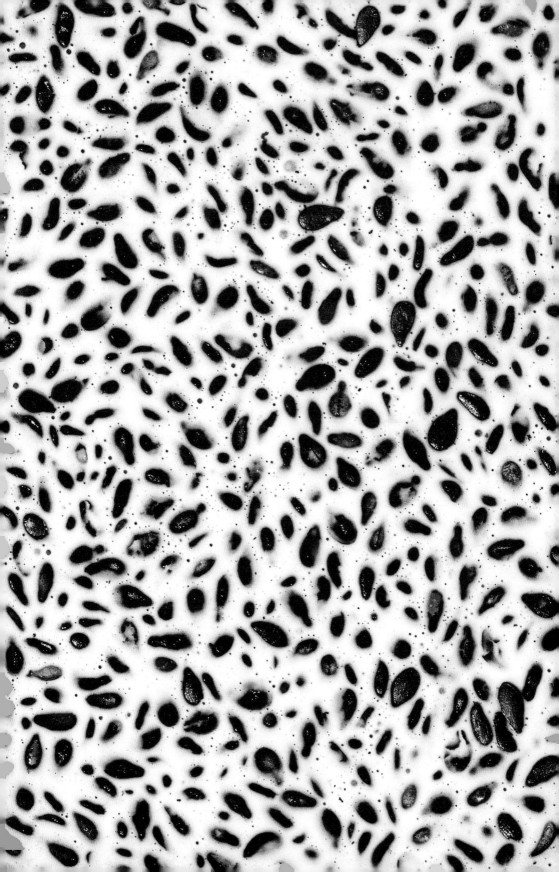